THE POTENTIAL OF
GLOBAL SUPPLY CHAINS
for Competitive Advantage

Ndubueze Kelvin Anyamele

Copyright © 2024 Ndubueze Kelvin Anyamele

All Rights Reserved.

The Potential of Global Supply Chains for Competitive Advantage

No portion of this book may be reproduced, stored, or shared in any form—whether electronic, mechanical, photocopying, recording, or via any other retrieval system—without express written permission from the copyright holder.

This publication is intended **solely for educational and informational purposes** and does not constitute financial or professional advice.

The author and publisher make no representations or warranties regarding the completeness, accuracy, or reliability of the content and do not endorse any third-party services, products, or links referenced herein.

Published Globally

ISBN: 978-9-1620-9161-3

Year of Publication: 2024

Publisher: Emphaloz Publishing House

A catalogue record for this publication is available from the National Library of Nigeria

Table Of Contents

Preface v

Introduction vii

CHAPTER ONE
Understanding the Foundations of Global Supply Chains 1

CHAPTER TWO
The Role of Globalization in Shaping Supply Chains 7

CHAPTER THREE
Key Elements of a High-Performance Supply Chain 15

CHAPTER FOUR
Supply Chain Strategy: Aligning with Business Goals 23

CHAPTER FIVE
Risk Management and Resilience in Global Supply Chains 31

CHAPTER SIX
Leveraging Technology for Supply Chain Innovation 37

CHAPTER SEVEN
Building a Sustainable and Ethical Supply Chain 45

CHAPTER EIGHT
The Importance of Supplier Relationships in Competitive Supply Chains -- 51

CHAPTER NINE
Sourcing and Procurement Strategies for Competitive Advantage 57

CHAPTER TEN
Global Logistics and Distribution: Overcoming Challenges 63

CHAPTER ELEVEN

Customer-Centric Supply Chains for Competitive Differentiation ------------ 71

CHAPTER TWELVE

Data-Driven Decision Making in Supply Chain Management ------------------ 77

CHAPTER THIRTEEN

The Role of Culture and Leadership in Supply Chain Success ----------------- 85

CHAPTER FOURTEEN

Measuring Supply Chain Performance and Continuous Improvement ------ 89

CHAPTER FIFTEEN

Future Trends in Global Supply Chain Management ---------------------------- 95

PREFACE

In an increasingly globalized world, businesses are no longer limited by geographic boundaries. Companies now source materials from one country, manufacture products in another, and sell to consumers worldwide. This transformation, driven by globalization, technological advancements, and evolving consumer demands, has made supply chains a central pillar of modern business strategy. But while supply chains have always been a critical function for ensuring products reach customers, the potential for these networks to become a strategic asset, driving competitive advantage, has only recently become fully apparent.

As businesses grow more interconnected, the complexity of managing global supply chains has increased. Where once supply chains were linear and localized, today they are sprawling, multifaceted systems that require coordination across multiple continents, regulatory environments, and cultures. This shift has introduced a unique set of challenges ranging from supply chain disruptions due to geopolitical tensions to sustainability pressures and the rapid adoption of new technologies. But with these challenges come tremendous opportunities for businesses willing to invest in their supply chain strategies.

This book, The Potential of Global Supply Chains for Competitive Advantage, is a response to the growing recognition that supply chains are not merely operational necessities, but powerful tools for business growth, agility, and differentiation. It seeks to provide insights, strategies, and frameworks that business leaders, supply chain managers, and students of business can use to harness the full potential of global supply chains.

Each chapter will delve into a different aspect of supply chain management, from foundational principles to advanced strategies, exploring how businesses can use their supply chains to reduce costs, increase efficiency, and, most importantly, gain a competitive edge in the marketplace. Through real-world examples and in-depth analysis, we will uncover how global supply chains can be transformed from cost centers into strategic assets that drive value and long-term success.

I have written this book not only for business professionals and academics but for anyone with an interest in understanding the profound impact that global supply chains have on business performance. It is my hope that the insights within these pages will inspire new ways of thinking about supply chain management and spark innovative approaches that will help businesses thrive in today's dynamic and highly competitive global economy.

INTRODUCTION

The global economy has evolved at an unprecedented pace in recent decades, driven by advances in technology, transportation, and communication. As a result, businesses are no longer confined to the boundaries of their home countries. Today, firms routinely operate across multiple continents, tapping into global markets for raw materials, labor, and consumers. At the heart of this globalized business environment are supply chains complex networks of suppliers, manufacturers, and distributors that work together to produce and deliver goods to the end customer.

But the role of global supply chains extends far beyond the efficient movement of products. In the modern business landscape, supply chains have emerged as critical drivers of competitive advantage. Companies that can effectively manage and optimize their supply chains often have a significant edge over their competitors. They can deliver products faster, reduce costs, maintain higher levels of quality, and respond more nimbly to changes in consumer demand or market conditions.

The purpose of this book is to explore how businesses can unlock the full potential of their global supply chains and use them to gain and sustain competitive advantage. We will explore the various components that make up a supply chain from sourcing and procurement to manufacturing and distribution and examine how each of these elements can be optimized for better performance. We will also delve into the broader strategic role that supply chains play in business, looking at how supply chain decisions can impact everything from customer satisfaction to innovation and market positioning.

Furthermore, this book will address some of the most pressing challenges facing global supply chains today. Supply chain disruptions, whether caused by natural disasters, geopolitical tensions, or pandemics, have shown just how vulnerable these networks can be. The rise of digital technologies like artificial intelligence (AI), blockchain, and the Internet of Things (IoT) has also created both opportunities and challenges for supply chain managers. And as consumers become more environmentally conscious, businesses are increasingly being called upon to develop more sustainable and ethical supply chains.

This book is structured to provide a comprehensive understanding of global supply chains and their role in business strategy. Each chapter will build on the last, providing practical insights and strategies that readers can apply to their own organizations. Whether you are a seasoned supply chain professional, a business leader looking to improve your company's operations, or a student of business strategy, this book will provide you with the tools you need to turn your supply chain into a competitive asset.

CHAPTER ONE
Understanding the Foundations of Global Supply Chains

Global supply chains are vast, interconnected systems that enable businesses to deliver goods and services to customers across the world. At their core, supply chains involve the flow of materials, information, and products from suppliers to manufacturers, and from manufacturers to customers. While the basic structure of a supply chain may seem straightforward producing and delivering products the actual dynamics that govern their operation are intricate, influenced by a range of factors such as geography, economics, politics, and technology.

To truly understand how modern global supply chain's function, it is essential to examine their historical roots and evolutionary trajectory. Supply chains have existed in some form for centuries, though they were much simpler than today's complex, multi-layered networks. In ancient times, supply chains were primarily confined to localized trade. However, with the development of long-distance trade routes like the Silk Road, merchants were able to exchange goods like silk, spices, and precious metals between Asia, Europe, and Africa. These early trade routes marked the beginning of supply chain management, though they were limited in both scale and scope, serving mainly a small elite of traders and consumers.

The Industrial Revolution, which began in the late 18th century, was a major turning point in the history of supply chains. With advancements in manufacturing and transportation technology such as the invention of the steam engine and the development of assembly lines businesses were able to produce goods on a larger scale and transport them more efficiently. These innovations laid the groundwork for the modern supply chain by increasing the complexity of production and distribution processes, which now spanned different regions and involved multiple stages. Manufacturing was no longer localized but spread across various locations depending on where raw materials were most accessible and labor most affordable.

The advent of globalization in the latter half of the 20th century further transformed supply chains, making them truly global in scope. As businesses sought to reduce costs and expand their customer base, they began to outsource production to countries with lower labor costs and more favorable regulatory environments. This shift gave rise to the modern global supply chains vast network of suppliers, manufacturers, and distributors that often spans multiple countries and continents. For example, a company headquartered in the United States might source raw materials from Southeast Asia, have the components manufactured in China, and then sell the final products in markets across Europe and North America.

Today, global supply chains are more interconnected and interdependent than ever before. While this interconnectedness has enabled businesses to reduce costs and tap into new markets, it has also introduced new levels of complexity. A typical supply chain now involves a web of suppliers, manufacturers, logistics providers, and distributors, all working together to deliver products to customers. Managing this intricate web requires a deep understanding of the various components that make up the supply chain, as well as the external forces such as changes in trade policies, shifts in consumer demand, and disruptions from natural disasters or geopolitical events that can impact its smooth operation.

One of the key challenges in managing a global supply chain is balancing efficiency with flexibility. Businesses strive to optimize their supply chains for cost efficiency, which often involves streamlining operations, negotiating favorable contracts with suppliers, and minimizing waste. However, these efforts to reduce costs must be carefully balanced against the need for flexibility. Supply chains must be able to adapt to market changes, such as fluctuations in consumer demand or disruptions in supply. For instance, a company might face challenges if one of its key suppliers is impacted by a natural disaster or if geopolitical events lead to trade restrictions. Achieving the right balance between efficiency and flexibility is critical for businesses looking to maintain their competitive edge in today's fast-paced global marketplace.

To achieve this balance, companies must engage in meticulous planning and adopt robust risk management strategies. A key aspect of this is building redundancies into the supply chain, such as maintaining relationships with multiple suppliers across different regions to mitigate the risk of disruption from any single source. Additionally, businesses need to invest in supply chain visibility, using advanced technology to track shipments, monitor inventory levels, and manage supplier relationships in real time. By having access to this data, supply chain managers can make informed decisions quickly and respond proactively to potential disruptions.

Technology has played a transformative role in the evolution of global supply chains. Over the past two decades, digital technologies have revolutionized supply chain management, allowing businesses to automate repetitive tasks, analyze vast amounts of data, and track shipments in real time. Technologies such as artificial intelligence (AI), blockchain, and the Internet of Things (IoT) have provided businesses with powerful tools to enhance efficiency, reduce costs, and improve customer service. For example, AI-powered predictive analytics can help companies forecast demand more accurately, reducing the risk of stockouts or overproduction. Blockchain technology, on the other hand, provides greater transparency and traceability in the supply chain by allowing businesses to verify the authenticity of products and ensure that they meet ethical and sustainability standards.

However, while technology provides significant advantages, it also presents new challenges. As businesses become more reliant on digital systems to manage their supply chains, they become more vulnerable to cyberattacks and data breaches. The risk of hackers gaining access to sensitive information, such as supplier contracts or shipping schedules, is an ever-present threat in today's digitized world. Moreover, the rapid pace of technological change means that businesses must continually invest in new systems and processes to stay competitive. Keeping up with these advancements can be costly, particularly for small and medium-sized enterprises that may not have the resources to invest in cutting-edge technologies.

Another critical consideration for businesses operating in global supply chains is sustainability. In recent years, consumers, investors, and governments have increasingly demanded that businesses adopt more sustainable practices throughout their supply chains. These demands are driven by growing awareness of environmental issues such as climate change, resource depletion, and pollution, as well as social issues like labor rights and fair wages. Businesses that fail to meet these expectations risk facing reputational damage, legal penalties, and loss of market share. For example, consumers are more likely to boycott brands that are associated with unethical labor practices or environmental harm, while investors may divest from companies that fail to adopt sustainable practices.

Sustainability, however, is not just a regulatory or ethical concern, it can also be a source of competitive advantage. Companies that prioritize sustainability in their supply chains can reduce costs, improve efficiency, and differentiate themselves from competitors. For example, adopting more energy-efficient manufacturing processes can lower operational costs while reducing a company's carbon footprint. Similarly, sourcing materials from ethical suppliers can enhance a company's brand image and build stronger relationships with customers who value corporate social responsibility. In some cases, sustainability initiatives can lead to innovation. For instance, the development of biodegradable packaging or the use of recycled materials in production can attract environmentally conscious consumers and open up new market opportunities.

In addition to sustainability, businesses must consider the ethical dimensions of their supply chains. Ethical supply chain management involves ensuring that all stakeholders suppliers, workers, and customers are treated fairly and with respect. This includes ensuring fair wages and safe working conditions for workers, particularly those in developing countries where labor laws may be less stringent. Ethical supply chains also focus on promoting diversity and inclusion, ensuring that suppliers reflect a range of cultural, racial, and gender perspectives. In today's socially conscious world, businesses that fail to uphold ethical standards in their supply chains may face backlash from consumers, activists, and regulatory bodies.

In conclusion, the foundations of global supply chains are built on a complex web of relationships and processes that span multiple countries, industries, and technologies. Managing these supply chains effectively requires a deep understanding of the various components that make up the supply chain, as well as the external forces that can impact its operation. By balancing efficiency with flexibility, embracing technological innovation, and prioritizing sustainability and ethical practices, businesses can build supply chains that are resilient, agile, and capable of delivering value to customers. Companies that can successfully navigate the complexities of global supply chains will be well-positioned to gain a competitive advantage in today's rapidly evolving global marketplace.

CHAPTER TWO
The Role of Globalization in Shaping Supply Chains

Globalization has fundamentally reshaped the way businesses operate, and at the heart of this transformation lies the global supply chain. Defined by the increasing interconnectedness of economies, cultures, and societies, globalization is driven by trade, investment, technology, and the movement of people. For businesses, globalization means the ability to establish networks that span continents sourcing raw materials from one country, manufacturing in another, and selling products to consumers across the globe. The role of globalization in supply chains is both profound and multifaceted, as it has opened up new opportunities for growth, efficiency, and innovation, while also presenting significant challenges in terms of complexity, risk management, and sustainability.

The concept of globalization has existed for centuries, but its modern form has evolved dramatically over the last few decades. Historically, most businesses operated within local or regional markets, relying on nearby suppliers and serving a limited customer base. Globalization began to take shape during the Age of Exploration in the 15th and 16th centuries, when European powers sought new trade routes to the East, giving rise to early forms of global trade. However, it was not until the late 20th century, with the advent of advanced transportation technologies, trade liberalization, and the rise of multinational corporations, that globalization truly accelerated, leading to the establishment of the intricate global supply chains we see today.

One of the most significant impacts of globalization on supply chains is the expansion of their geographic reach. Previously, businesses were confined to sourcing materials and components from suppliers located within their domestic markets. However, as transportation technologies improved and trade barriers were lowered, companies began to look beyond their borders for cost savings and growth opportunities. This trend led to the rise of global supply chains, where companies source materials from countries with lower labor costs, manufacture goods in regions with specialized expertise, and distribute products to consumers worldwide. For example, a company based in the United States might source raw materials from Brazil, manufacture products in China, and sell them across Europe and Asia.

The expansion of supply chains across borders has provided businesses with access to a broader pool of resources, suppliers, and talent. One of the primary advantages of globalization is the ability to source materials and labor from regions where they are most abundant or cost-effective. This approach, known as comparative advantage, allows businesses to optimize their supply chains by reducing production costs while improving efficiency. For instance, a company that manufactures electronics might source rare earth metals from Africa, where these resources are abundant, while outsourcing labor-intensive production to countries in Southeast Asia, where labor costs are lower. This strategy enables companies to maintain competitive pricing while maximizing their profit margins.

In addition to cost savings, globalization has opened up new markets for businesses, allowing them to reach a much larger customer base than would be possible if they only operated domestically. By establishing global supply chains, companies can distribute their products to consumers in multiple regions, tapping into diverse markets with varying demand patterns. This is particularly important for industries like consumer electronics, fashion, and automotive, where demand is global, and customer preferences vary across regions. For example, a car manufacturer might design vehicles tailored to the specific needs and preferences of customers in Europe, North America, and Asia, while leveraging global supply chains to source parts and components from different regions.

However, while globalization offers significant opportunities for growth and efficiency, it also introduces new complexities into supply chain management. One of the primary challenges is the increased complexity of supply chain networks. As supply chains become more geographically dispersed, the number of suppliers, manufacturers, and logistics providers involved in the production and delivery of goods increases, making it more difficult for businesses to monitor and control every aspect of the supply chain. This complexity can lead to risks such as quality control issues, delays, and disruptions, all of which can have a negative impact on a company's ability to meet customer demand.

Another challenge of globalization is the increased risk of supply chain disruptions due to geopolitical tensions, trade wars, or natural disasters. For example, a company that relies heavily on raw materials from a single country may face significant supply shortages if that country experiences political instability, natural disasters, or changes in trade policy. Similarly, tariffs and trade restrictions imposed by governments can disrupt the flow of goods across borders, increase costs for businesses, and create uncertainty in the supply chain.

The COVID-19 pandemic provided a stark reminder of the vulnerability of global supply chains, as many businesses experienced significant disruptions due to factory shutdowns, border closures, and constrained transportation networks.

In response to these challenges, businesses must adopt more robust risk management strategies to ensure the resilience of their supply chains. One effective approach is to diversify suppliers and manufacturers across different regions, reducing reliance on any single country or region for critical materials or components. For instance, a company that sources raw materials from Southeast Asia might establish secondary suppliers in Africa or South America to mitigate the risk of supply disruptions. This diversification strategy allows businesses to maintain continuity in the event of geopolitical or environmental disruptions, ensuring that their supply chains remain resilient in the face of uncertainty.

Technology plays a crucial role in managing the complexities of global supply chains. Advances in digital technologies, such as blockchain, artificial intelligence (AI), and the Internet of Things (IoT), have provided businesses with new tools to monitor and optimize their supply chains in real time. For example, IoT devices can be used to track shipments, monitor inventory levels, and predict potential delays in the delivery of goods. By providing real-time visibility into supply chain operations, these technologies allow businesses to make data-driven decisions, improving efficiency and reducing the risk of disruptions. Blockchain technology, in particular, is revolutionizing supply chain transparency by providing a secure, tamper-proof record of every transaction, enabling businesses to verify the authenticity of products and ensure compliance with ethical and sustainability standards.

Globalization has also increased the importance of sustainability in supply chain management. As businesses expand their global supply chains, they are under increasing pressure from consumers, investors, and regulators to ensure that their operations are environmentally and socially responsible. Sustainability is no longer a niche concern but a mainstream business imperative, with consumers demanding that companies adopt sustainable practices throughout their supply chains, from sourcing materials to manufacturing and distribution. For example, companies in the fashion industry are under increasing scrutiny to reduce the environmental impact of their supply chains, particularly in terms of water usage, carbon emissions, and waste generated during production.

Businesses that fail to meet these sustainability expectations risk damaging their reputations and losing market share to competitors that prioritize environmental and social responsibility. On the other hand, companies that integrate sustainability into their global supply chains can differentiate themselves from competitors and build stronger relationships with customers who value ethical practices. In many cases, sustainability initiatives can also lead to cost savings and operational efficiencies. For example, by adopting energy-efficient manufacturing processes or optimizing transportation routes to reduce fuel consumption, businesses can lower operational costs while reducing their environmental impact.

Furthermore, globalization has driven innovation in supply chain management. The interconnected nature of global supply chains has allowed businesses to collaborate with suppliers, manufacturers, and logistics providers from different parts of the world to improve processes, reduce lead times, and enhance product quality. For example, a company might work with its suppliers to develop innovative packaging solutions that reduce shipping costs and environmental impact. Similarly, manufacturers can collaborate with logistics providers to streamline transportation and reduce the time it takes to move goods from one part of the world to another. This collaborative approach to supply chain management not only improves efficiency but also fosters innovation, allowing businesses to remain competitive in an increasingly globalized market.

However, managing global supply chains requires businesses to navigate a complex web of logistical, regulatory, and cultural challenges. Each country has its own set of regulations, tariffs, and customs procedures, which can vary significantly from one region to another. For example, products that meet regulatory standards in the European Union may require different certifications for sale in the United States or China. Navigating these regulatory environments requires careful planning, as businesses must ensure that their products comply with local laws and standards while avoiding delays at customs.

Cultural differences also play a significant role in global supply chain management. For instance, business practices, communication styles, and negotiation tactics can vary widely between countries. A company that is accustomed to doing business in North America may face challenges when dealing with suppliers in Asia, where relationship-building and face-to-face meetings are often considered more important than formal contracts. Understanding these cultural nuances is essential for building strong relationships with global suppliers and ensuring smooth operations.

In conclusion, globalization has transformed the way businesses manage their supply chains, offering new opportunities for growth, efficiency, and innovation. By expanding supply chains across borders, companies can access new markets, reduce costs, and collaborate with global partners to drive innovation. However, globalization also presents significant challenges, including increased complexity, supply chain disruptions, and the need for sustainability. To succeed in this globalized environment, businesses must adopt robust risk management strategies, leverage advanced technologies, and prioritize sustainability in their supply chains. Companies that can navigate the complexities of globalization while optimizing their supply chains for efficiency, resilience, and sustainability will be well-positioned to gain a competitive advantage in the global marketplace.

Ndubueze Kelvin Anyamele

CHAPTER THREE
Key Elements of a High-Performance Supply Chain

A high-performance supply chain is essential for businesses to thrive in today's fast-paced, competitive global marketplace. Companies that can effectively manage their supply chains are able to deliver products faster, reduce costs, and provide superior customer service. However, building and maintaining a high-performance supply chain is a complex task that involves optimizing numerous interrelated components, from sourcing and procurement to logistics and distribution. These elements must be aligned with a company's strategic objectives and adapted to the unique challenges of the industries in which they operate.

A high-performance supply chain requires the integration of multiple functions, the collaboration of various stakeholders, and the continuous monitoring of performance metrics. It must not only function efficiently in normal conditions but also be resilient enough to adapt to disruptions and changes in market conditions. The most successful companies are those that manage to create agile, flexible supply chains that can respond quickly to fluctuations in demand, supply chain disruptions, and evolving customer preferences.

One of the most critical elements of a high-performance supply chain is sourcing and procurement. These functions form the foundation of the supply chain, as they determine where a company obtains the raw materials, components, and services it needs to manufacture its products. Effective sourcing and procurement are vital to ensuring that the right materials are available at the right time and at the right price. For businesses operating in a global environment, sourcing and procurement can be a particularly complex process, as they involve navigating different regulatory environments, varying cultural practices, and logistical challenges.

To optimize sourcing and procurement, businesses need to focus on developing strong, long-term relationships with their suppliers. Supplier relationships are no longer viewed as purely transactional; rather, they are seen as strategic partnerships that can provide a competitive advantage. Companies that collaborate closely with their suppliers can negotiate better terms, improve the quality of materials, and reduce costs. These partnerships often involve joint initiatives to streamline production processes, improve sustainability practices, and innovate new products. By fostering strong supplier relationships, businesses can create a more reliable, efficient, and resilient supply chain that is better equipped to respond to changes in market demand or unexpected disruptions.

Additionally, procurement strategies have shifted from focusing solely on cost to balancing cost with value. While securing the lowest price for raw materials or components remains important, companies are increasingly prioritizing other factors, such as supplier reliability, quality, and sustainability. For example, a company may choose to work with a supplier that offers more sustainable materials or better labor practices, even if it comes at a higher cost. These considerations not only help businesses reduce risks but also enhance their brand reputation and align with the growing consumer demand for ethically sourced products.

Another vital element of a high-performance supply chain is logistics and transportation. Once raw materials or finished products are sourced, they must be moved efficiently through the supply chain, whether it's from a supplier to a manufacturing facility, from a manufacturing facility to a distribution center, or directly to customers. Efficient logistics and transportation are crucial for ensuring that products are delivered on time, in the right condition, and at the lowest possible cost.

Global logistics present significant challenges due to the need to coordinate the movement of goods across multiple countries, transportation modes, and regulatory environments. Businesses must account for customs procedures, tariffs, and compliance with international trade laws, all of which can introduce delays and add costs to the process. Moreover, geopolitical events, such as trade wars, sanctions, and transportation disruptions due to natural disasters, can exacerbate these challenges.

To optimize logistics and transportation, businesses must invest in technology that provides real-time visibility into the movement of goods throughout the supply chain. Technologies such as GPS tracking, predictive analytics, and IoT sensors allow companies to monitor shipments in real time, identify potential delays, and make adjustments to shipping routes to ensure timely delivery. Predictive analytics can also help businesses anticipate demand fluctuations, enabling them to adjust inventory levels and transportation schedules proactively. Automation in transportation management systems (TMS) helps streamline operations by optimizing shipping routes, reducing lead times, and minimizing transportation costs.

Moreover, innovations such as autonomous vehicles and drones are beginning to play a role in improving last-mile delivery, which is often the most expensive and challenging aspect of logistics. By automating the delivery process and using advanced algorithms to plan the most efficient routes, businesses can reduce the time and cost associated with delivering products to customers.

Inventory management is another critical component of a high-performance supply chain. Managing inventory effectively is essential for ensuring that businesses have enough stock to meet customer demand while avoiding the costs associated with overstocking or stockouts. A company's ability to strike this balance directly impacts its profitability, cash flow, and customer satisfaction. If a company holds too much inventory, it ties up valuable capital and incurs additional storage costs. On the other hand, if inventory levels are too low, the company risks running out of stock, leading to missed sales opportunities, delayed orders, and dissatisfied customers.

In today's dynamic market environment, businesses need to implement sophisticated inventory management systems that provide real-time visibility into inventory levels across the entire supply chain. These systems use advanced technologies such as RFID (radio-frequency identification) tags, IoT devices, and AI-driven demand forecasting models to track the movement of goods and predict future demand accurately. By leveraging these technologies, companies can reduce excess inventory, improve cash flow, and minimize the risk of stockouts.

One strategy that businesses often use to optimize inventory management is the just-in-time (JIT) approach. JIT inventory management aims to minimize the amount of inventory held by delivering materials and products exactly when they are needed in the production process or to fulfill customer orders. This approach reduces storage costs and waste, as companies avoid holding excess stock. However, JIT requires a highly efficient and reliable supply chain, as any delays in the delivery of materials or components can disrupt production. For JIT to succeed, businesses need strong relationships with suppliers and robust logistics systems that can ensure timely deliveries.

Manufacturing and production processes are also key elements of a high-performance supply chain. Efficient manufacturing practices enable companies to produce high-quality products quickly, at a lower cost, and in response to fluctuating customer demand. Today, businesses are increasingly adopting advanced manufacturing technologies, such as automation, robotics, and 3D printing, to enhance productivity, reduce labor costs, and minimize production errors. For example, in the automotive industry, robots are commonly used on production lines to assemble vehicles with greater speed and precision than human workers. Similarly, 3D printing technology is revolutionizing the production of customized products by allowing businesses to manufacture goods on demand, reducing the need for large inventories of finished products.

Lean manufacturing principles are another key aspect of high-performance production systems. Lean manufacturing focuses on eliminating waste, optimizing resources, and improving efficiency. By identifying inefficiencies in the production process and implementing continuous improvement practices, businesses can reduce lead times, lower production costs, and improve product quality. The lean approach also emphasizes cross-functional collaboration, with teams from different departments working together to identify and solve problems, streamline processes, and improve overall supply chain performance.

Customer service is the final, yet equally critical, element of a high-performance supply chain. In today's consumer-driven marketplace, businesses must be able to respond quickly and efficiently to customer needs. Meeting customer expectations requires a supply chain that is both flexible and responsive, capable of adjusting to changes in demand, offering personalized products, and providing accurate information on order status and delivery times. Companies that prioritize customer service in their supply chain management are better positioned to enhance customer satisfaction, build loyalty, and drive long-term growth.

To optimize customer service, businesses must integrate their supply chain operations with customer-facing technologies, such as order management systems, customer relationship management (CRM) software, and real-time tracking tools. These technologies provide customers with the transparency they expect, allowing them to track their orders, view estimated delivery times, and communicate with customer service representatives in real time. Additionally, businesses must ensure that their supply chains are agile enough to accommodate last-minute changes, such as expedited shipping requests or changes in order quantities, without sacrificing efficiency or increasing costs.

In recent years, omnichannel retailing has further complicated the challenge of managing customer service in supply chains. Omnichannel retailing involves providing a seamless shopping experience across multiple platforms, including online stores, mobile apps, and brick-and-mortar locations. To meet the demands of omnichannel customers, businesses need to integrate their supply chains with their sales channels, ensuring that inventory is available across all platforms and that products can be delivered quickly, regardless of where the order is placed. This requires sophisticated inventory management systems, seamless coordination between different parts of the supply chain, and the ability to fulfill orders from various distribution centers or retail locations.

In conclusion, building and maintaining a high-performance supply chain requires businesses to optimize several interconnected elements, including sourcing and procurement, logistics and transportation, inventory management, manufacturing and production, and customer service. By focusing on these areas, businesses can create supply chains that are agile, efficient, and responsive to the ever-changing demands of the global marketplace. In today's competitive environment, a high-performance supply chain is not just a necessity it is a key source of competitive advantage. Companies that invest in their supply chain capabilities will be better equipped to navigate the complexities of global trade, meet customer expectations, and achieve long-term success.

Ndubueze Kelvin Anyamele

CHAPTER FOUR
Supply Chain Strategy: Aligning with Business Goals

In today's competitive and dynamic business landscape, supply chains are no longer merely logistical systems designed to deliver products from point A to point B. Instead, they have evolved into strategic assets that play a central role in achieving a company's long-term goals. Businesses that successfully align their supply chain strategies with their overarching business objectives are better positioned to thrive, especially in industries where efficiency, innovation, and the ability to respond quickly to changing market conditions are crucial.

Supply chain strategy alignment involves ensuring that every part of the supply chain supports the company's broader goals whether those goals are focused on cost leadership, customer service excellence, innovation, sustainability, or market expansion. When supply chain strategy and business goals are misaligned, businesses risk losing competitiveness, missing opportunities for growth, and incurring unnecessary costs. On the other hand, companies that tailor their supply chain strategies to their specific business objectives can turn their supply chains into powerful engines of competitive advantage.

The starting point for aligning supply chain strategy with business goals is to clearly define the company's overall strategic objectives. These objectives vary depending on the company's industry, competitive landscape, and target market. For example, a company competing with cost leadership will require a supply chain focused on maximizing efficiency, reducing costs, and minimizing waste. Conversely, a company that competes on differentiation offering unique, high-value products will need a more flexible, responsive supply chain capable of delivering customized products and superior customer service. Regardless of the business model, the first step is understanding what the business is trying to achieve and ensuring that the supply chain is structured to support these goals.

A critical aspect of aligning supply chain strategy with business goals is adopting a customer-centric approach. While internal efficiencies are important, the ultimate goal of the supply chain is to meet and exceed customer expectations. Companies that focus solely on optimizing their internal processes without considering the customer experience may find themselves delivering products efficiently but failing to meet customer demands. In many cases, customer dissatisfaction results from supply chain failures whether it's stockouts, late deliveries, or poor product quality. Therefore, a truly aligned supply chain must be designed with the customer in mind.

To achieve this alignment, companies need to segment their supply chains based on the different types of products they offer or the varying needs of their customer base. This segmentation allows businesses to create tailored supply chain strategies that address the specific requirements of each segment. For instance, a company that offers both high-volume, low-margin products and low-volume, high-margin products may adopt different supply chain strategies for each segment. High-volume products may be routed through highly efficient, cost-optimized supply chains, while low-volume, high-margin products may require a more flexible supply chain that can handle customization, shorter lead times, and superior customer service. By segmenting their supply chains, companies can optimize operations for different product categories and customer demands.

Flexibility and agility are also essential elements of an aligned supply chain strategy. In today's fast-paced and unpredictable business environment, supply chains must be adaptable and capable of responding quickly to changes in market conditions. For instance, fluctuations in customer demand, sudden shifts in raw material prices, or supply chain disruptions due to geopolitical events can have significant impacts on supply chain performance. A rigid supply chain that is unable to adjust to these changes can result in inefficiencies, higher costs, and lost sales. Therefore, companies need to build flexibility and agility into their supply chains to ensure they can respond effectively to unexpected events and capitalize on new opportunities.

Building a flexible supply chain requires investments in both technology and processes that provide real-time visibility into every aspect of the supply chain. Real-time visibility is critical for identifying potential problems, such as delays in shipments, inventory shortages, or changes in demand, before they escalate into significant issues. Technologies such as advanced analytics, artificial intelligence (AI), and the Internet of Things (IoT) enable businesses to monitor supply chain performance in real time, predict potential disruptions, and make data-driven decisions that improve responsiveness and agility. For example, AI-powered demand forecasting tools can help companies anticipate changes in customer demand and adjust production schedules, inventory levels, and shipping routes accordingly.

A strategic approach to collaboration is another important aspect of aligning supply chain strategy with business goals. In today's interconnected global marketplace, no company operates in isolation. Supply chains are complex networks that involve suppliers, manufacturers, logistics providers, and customers, all of whom must work together to ensure the smooth flow of goods. Collaboration between these stakeholders is essential for creating an efficient and effective supply chain.

One-way businesses can enhance collaboration by sharing data and information with key partners. For example, companies can share demand forecasts, inventory levels, and production schedules with their suppliers, allowing suppliers to plan their operations more effectively and ensure they can meet the company's needs. Similarly, businesses can collaborate with logistics providers to optimize transportation routes, reduce lead times, and lower costs. By fostering a culture of collaboration and transparency, businesses can create more resilient and efficient supply chains that are better able to adapt to market changes.

Another critical factor in aligning supply chain strategy with business goals is risk management. As supply chains become more global and complex, they are exposed to a wide range of risks, from natural disasters and geopolitical events to cyberattacks and supplier failures. A supply chain disruption can have severe consequences, including lost sales, increased costs, and damage to the company's reputation. Therefore, businesses must adopt robust risk management strategies that help them anticipate, mitigate, and recover from supply chain disruptions.

One effective risk management strategy is supplier diversification. Relying on a single supplier or a single geographic region for critical materials or components exposes businesses to significant risks. For example, if a company relies on a single supplier in a region prone to natural disasters, it may face supply shortages if that region is hit by a hurricane or earthquake. By diversifying suppliers and establishing relationships with multiple suppliers across different regions, businesses can reduce their exposure to these risks and ensure continuity in the event of a disruption. Additionally, companies should regularly assess the risk profiles of their suppliers and develop contingency plans to address potential supply chain disruptions.

Sustainability is another key consideration when aligning supply chain strategy with business goals. In recent years, there has been growing pressure from consumers, investors, and regulators for businesses to adopt more sustainable practices in their supply chains. Sustainability is no longer a "nice to have" but a critical component of long-term business success. Companies that prioritize sustainability in their supply chains can reduce costs, improve efficiency, and enhance their brand reputation. For example, businesses that reduce waste, lower carbon emissions, or source materials from ethical suppliers can differentiate themselves from competitors and appeal to environmentally conscious consumers.

A sustainable supply chain is not only beneficial from a branding perspective but can also lead to significant operational efficiencies. For instance, reducing energy consumption in manufacturing facilities or optimizing transportation routes to reduce fuel consumption can result in lower operational costs. Additionally, companies that prioritize sustainability are often better positioned to comply with regulatory requirements, avoiding fines or penalties for non-compliance with environmental regulations.

To successfully align supply chain strategy with sustainability goals, businesses need to establish clear sustainability metrics and track their progress over time. These metrics may include carbon emissions, energy consumption, waste reduction, and water usage, among others. By regularly monitoring these metrics, companies can identify areas for improvement and implement initiatives to reduce their environmental impact.

In addition to aligning with sustainability objectives, businesses must ensure that their supply chain strategies are aligned with the company's competitive positioning in the market. For example, a company that competes on innovation and product differentiation will need a supply chain that supports rapid product development, customization, and speed to market. In contrast, a company that competes on price leadership will need a supply chain focused on cost reduction, efficiency, and scalability.

Aligning supply chain strategy with competitive positioning involves carefully analyzing market trends, customer preferences, and the actions of competitors. By understanding the competitive landscape, companies can design supply chains that not only meet current market demands but also position the business for future growth. For example, a company that anticipates rising demand for sustainable products can invest in supply chain capabilities that support the development and delivery of eco-friendly products, gaining an advantage over competitors that are slower to adopt sustainability practices.

Finally, continuous improvement is essential for maintaining alignment between supply chain strategy and business goals. The business environment is constantly evolving, and companies must regularly assess and refine their supply chain strategies to ensure they remain competitive. This requires ongoing performance monitoring, the use of key performance indicators (KPIs), and a commitment to continuous improvement. KPIs such as inventory turnover, order lead times, on-time delivery rates, and customer satisfaction scores provide valuable insights into supply chain performance and highlight areas where improvements can be made.

In conclusion, aligning supply chain strategy with business goals is essential for companies that want to gain a competitive advantage in today's global marketplace. This alignment requires a clear understanding of the company's strategic objectives, a customer-centric approach to supply chain design, and the ability to respond quickly to changes in the market. Businesses must also prioritize collaboration with external partners, adopt robust risk management strategies, and integrate sustainability into their supply chain operations. By continuously monitoring performance and making data-driven decisions, companies can create supply chains that support their business goals, drive innovation, and position themselves for long-term success in a rapidly changing global environment.

Ndubueze Kelvin Anyamele

CHAPTER FIVE
Risk Management and Resilience in Global Supply Chains

Risk management and resilience have become two of the most critical components in the effective management of global supply chains. In today's volatile world, businesses are faced with a wide range of potential disruptions that can impact their ability to deliver goods and services to customers. These disruptions can arise from a variety of sources, including natural disasters, geopolitical tensions, economic instability, cyberattacks, supplier failures, and even global pandemics like COVID-19. As a result, the importance of developing robust strategies to mitigate these risks and build resilient supply chains that can adapt to and recover from unexpected events has never been more pronounced.

In this chapter, we will explore the different types of risks that can affect global supply chains, and we will discuss strategies for mitigating these risks. We will also examine the concept of supply chain resilience and provide practical insights into how businesses can build supply chains that are capable of withstanding and recovering from disruptions. By proactively managing risks and investing in resilience, companies can better protect themselves from the uncertainties of the global marketplace and ensure that they continue to deliver value to their customers, even in the face of unexpected challenges.

The first step in effective risk management is identifying the potential risks that a company's supply chain may face. These risks can be broadly categorized into several types: operational risks, financial risks, environmental risks, and cybersecurity risks. Each category presents unique challenges and requires tailored strategies for mitigation.

Operational risks refer to the risks that arise from the day-to-day functioning of the supply chain. These include disruptions caused by supplier failures, transportation delays, equipment breakdowns, or labor strikes. While operational risks are often localized, they can have a cascading effect on the entire supply chain if not managed properly. For example, a delay in the delivery of raw materials from a supplier can lead to production stoppages, which in turn can delay the delivery of finished goods to customers. Similarly, labor strikes at ports or manufacturing facilities can bring entire supply chains to a halt. Businesses need to continuously monitor their supply chain operations and work closely with suppliers and logistics providers to address potential operational risks as they arise.

Financial risks are another important category of risks that can significantly impact global supply chains. These include risks related to currency fluctuations, changes in trade policies, shifts in interest rates, and fluctuations in commodity prices. For businesses that operate across multiple countries, exchange rate fluctuations can have a significant impact on the cost of goods and materials. For example, a sudden depreciation in the local currency of a supplier's country can increase the cost of imports, eroding profit margins. Additionally, changes in tariffs or trade regulations, such as those introduced during trade wars, can increase costs or restrict access to certain markets, forcing companies to reconsider their sourcing strategies. Businesses that operate globally must adopt currency hedging strategies, diversify their financial exposure, and stay informed about regulatory changes to minimize the impact of financial risks on their supply chains.

Environmental risks are some of the most unpredictable and potentially devastating risks to global supply chains. These risks include natural disasters, climate change, and global pandemics. Natural disasters such as earthquakes, hurricanes, floods, and wildfires can disrupt entire regions, halting production and distribution for extended periods of time. The COVID-19 pandemic, for example, disrupted supply chains on a global scale, with factory shutdowns, border closures, and severe transportation constraints leading to widespread delays and shortages. Climate change is also having an increasingly significant impact on supply chains, such as rising temperatures, changing weather patterns, and more frequent extreme weather events disrupt the production and distribution of goods. Businesses must consider the long-term effects of climate change on their supply chains and develop strategies to mitigate these risks, such as investing in climate-resilient infrastructure and sourcing materials from regions less vulnerable to environmental risks.

Cybersecurity risks are becoming an increasingly critical concern for global supply chains as businesses adopt more digital technologies and rely on interconnected systems. Cyberattacks can target key systems such as inventory management software, transportation tracking systems, or supplier databases, leading to significant disruptions in the supply chain. A cyberattack on a single supplier or logistics provider can have far-reaching consequences, potentially halting production, delaying shipments, and compromising sensitive data. To mitigate cybersecurity risks, businesses must invest in robust cybersecurity measures, including encryption, multi-factor authentication, and regular vulnerability assessments. Additionally, businesses should ensure that their supply chain partners adhere to the same security standards, as weaknesses in a partner's system can create vulnerabilities in the entire supply chain.

To effectively manage these risks, companies must develop comprehensive risk management strategies that are tailored to the specific risks they face. One of the most common strategies for managing supply chain risks is diversification. By diversifying suppliers, production facilities, and distribution networks, companies can reduce their reliance on any single source or location. For example, a company that relies heavily on a single supplier for critical materials may choose to source these materials from multiple suppliers in different regions. This way, if one supplier is unable to deliver due to a natural disaster or geopolitical event, the company can still rely on other suppliers to meet its needs. Diversification not only reduces the impact of disruptions but also provides companies with greater flexibility in adjusting to changes in the market or shifts in demand.

Another key strategy for managing supply chain risks is building strong relationships with suppliers and other key partners. Collaboration and open communication are essential for identifying potential risks early and developing strategies to mitigate them. Companies that have strong relationships with their suppliers are often able to work together to address issues such as production delays, transportation disruptions, or regulatory changes before they impact the broader supply chain. Additionally, long-term partnerships with suppliers allow businesses to jointly invest in risk mitigation strategies, such as improving quality control measures or enhancing cybersecurity protocols.

In addition to managing risks, companies must also focus on building resilient supply chains that can adapt to and recover from disruptions. Supply chain resilience refers to the ability of a supply chain to continue functioning in the face of unexpected events, and to recover quickly once a disruption has occurred. A resilient supply chain is flexible, agile, and able to respond quickly to changes in demand, supply, or other external factors. Building resilience requires businesses to invest in the infrastructure, technology, and processes that enable them to adapt to changing circumstances and recover from disruptions with minimal impact on their operations.

One of the key elements of supply chain resilience is redundancy. While redundancy may seem counterintuitive to efficiency, having backup suppliers, production facilities, and transportation routes can help ensure that a company's operations continue even in the event of a disruption. For example, a company that manufactures its products in multiple locations can continue production at one facility if another is forced to shut down due to a natural disaster. Similarly, businesses that maintain relationships with multiple logistics providers or transportation carriers can reroute shipments in the event of a transportation disruption, ensuring that products reach customers on time.

Technology also plays a critical role in building resilient supply chains. Advances in data analytics, artificial intelligence (AI), and automation have made it possible for businesses to monitor their supply chains in real time and respond more quickly to potential disruptions. For example, companies can use predictive analytics to forecast potential risks, such as weather events or supply shortages, and take proactive steps to mitigate these risks. Predictive analytics tools analyze historical data and current market trends to identify patterns and predict future disruptions, allowing businesses to prepare contingency plans in advance. Similarly, automation can help reduce the impact of labor shortages or production slowdowns by enabling companies to continue operating even with reduced staff. Automated systems can perform routine tasks such as inventory management, order processing, and quality control with minimal human intervention, ensuring that supply chain operations remain efficient even during periods of disruption.

Finally, companies must focus on developing a culture of resilience within their organizations. This involves training employees to identify potential risks, developing contingency plans for various types of disruptions, and fostering a mindset of agility and adaptability. Businesses that prioritize resilience are better able to respond to disruptions and recover more quickly, minimizing the impact on their operations and maintaining their competitive advantage. Creating a culture of resilience also requires strong leadership, as executives must be committed to investing in risk management and resilience-building initiatives, even when the short-term benefits may not be immediately apparent.

In conclusion, risk management and resilience are critical components of global supply chain management. By identifying potential risks, developing strategies to mitigate these risks, and building resilient supply chains that can adapt to disruptions, businesses can protect themselves from the many uncertainties of the global marketplace. In doing so, they can ensure that they continue to deliver value to their customers, even in the face of unexpected challenges. Companies that invest in risk management and resilience are not only better positioned to withstand disruptions but also to capitalize on new opportunities as they arise, giving them a competitive edge in an increasingly complex and unpredictable world.

CHAPTER SIX
Leveraging Technology for Supply Chain Innovation

In the modern business landscape, technology has become a driving force behind innovation, particularly in the realm of supply chain management. The increasing complexity of global supply chains, combined with rapidly evolving consumer demands, has led companies to adopt technological solutions to improve efficiency, enhance visibility, and reduce costs. The convergence of advancements in artificial intelligence (AI), machine learning, blockchain, and the Internet of Things (IoT) has provided businesses with powerful tools to optimize their supply chain operations, enabling them to gain a competitive edge in an increasingly interconnected world.

Technology is reshaping supply chains by automating processes, improving decision-making, enhancing transparency, and fostering more agile, customer-centric operations. In this chapter, we will explore how businesses can leverage technology to innovate and transform their supply chains. We will examine some of the most significant technological advancements in supply chain management and discuss how these innovations can be applied to streamline operations, improve forecasting, reduce waste, and drive overall supply chain performance.

One of the most profound impacts of technology on supply chain management is in the field of data analytics and predictive modeling. Supply chains generate vast amounts of data at every stage, from sourcing raw materials and managing production schedules to coordinating shipping and monitoring delivery times. Historically, much of this data was fragmented and difficult to analyze in real-time, making it challenging for businesses to make informed decisions quickly. However, the rise of big data analytics has revolutionized this landscape. Today, companies can collect, analyze, and act on data from every touchpoint in their supply chain, gaining valuable insights into areas such as demand forecasting, inventory management, supplier performance, and transportation logistics.

Predictive analytics is one of the most powerful applications of data analytics in supply chain management. By analyzing historical data and applying advanced algorithms, companies can forecast future trends, anticipate disruptions, and make more accurate decisions about inventory levels, production schedules, and shipping routes. For example, a retailer might use predictive analytics to forecast consumer demand for specific products during the holiday season, allowing them to adjust inventory levels accordingly and avoid the risks of stockouts or overstocking. This proactive approach to managing inventory helps optimize cash flow, reduce waste, and ensure that products are available when and where customers need them.

Machine learning, a subset of AI, further enhances the predictive capabilities of supply chains by continuously learning from data and improving its predictive accuracy over time. Machine learning algorithms can analyze patterns in supplier performance, transportation delays, and customer behavior, allowing businesses to adjust procurement schedules or reroute shipments based on real-time insights. For example, machine learning can predict the likelihood of a supplier missing a deadline based on past performance data, enabling companies to take preemptive action by placing orders earlier or sourcing from alternative suppliers. This level of automation reduces the need for manual intervention, allowing supply chain managers to focus on higher-level strategic tasks and decision-making.

Another significant technological advancement in supply chain management is the Internet of Things (IoT). IoT refers to a network of connected devices ranging from sensors and smart tags to vehicles and machinery that communicate and share data in real-time. In a supply chain context, IoT technology can be used to monitor the location, condition, and movement of goods throughout the supply chain, from production facilities to distribution centers to the final delivery at the customer's doorstep.

For example, IoT-enabled sensors placed on shipping containers can provide real-time updates on the temperature and humidity levels inside, ensuring that perishable goods, such as food or pharmaceuticals, are transported under optimal conditions. If the sensors detect a deviation from the required conditions, the system can automatically trigger alerts, allowing supply chain managers to take corrective action before the goods are spoiled. This enhanced level of visibility and control improves product quality, reduces waste, and ensures compliance with regulatory requirements, particularly in industries with stringent safety and quality standards.

IoT also plays a key role in inventory management. By using RFID (Radio Frequency Identification) tags and sensors, businesses can track the movement of goods in real-time and monitor inventory levels across multiple locations. This allows companies to have a clear and accurate view of their inventory at any given moment, reducing the likelihood of stockouts or excess inventory. For example, in a large warehouse, IoT-enabled systems can automatically update inventory records as products move through different stages of the supply chain, providing accurate, real-time data on stock levels. This reduces the need for manual stocktaking, improves efficiency, and allows for more responsive supply chain operations.

Blockchain technology is another transformative innovation that is reshaping supply chain management, particularly in terms of improving transparency, security, and traceability. Blockchain is a decentralized digital ledger that records transactions in a secure, immutable manner. In the context of supply chains, blockchain can be used to create a transparent and tamper-proof record of every transaction, from the sourcing of raw materials to the final delivery of finished products. This level of transparency is invaluable in industries where authenticity, ethical sourcing, and compliance are critical.

One of the most significant benefits of blockchain technology in supply chains is its ability to enhance traceability. In industries such as food and pharmaceuticals, where safety and quality are paramount, blockchain enables companies to trace the origin and movement of products throughout the supply chain. For example, in the event of a foodborne illness outbreak, blockchain technology can be used to quickly trace the affected products back to their source, allowing companies to isolate the contaminated items and prevent further distribution. This rapid traceability not only protects consumers but also minimizes the financial and reputational damage to the company.

Blockchain also helps improve trust and accountability in supply chains by providing a secure, transparent record of every transaction. In global supply chains, where businesses often deal with multiple suppliers and partners across different countries and regulatory environments, blockchain technology can be used to verify the authenticity of goods, ensure that they meet ethical sourcing standards, and confirm compliance with regulatory requirements. This reduces the risk of fraud, counterfeiting, and supply chain disruptions, providing greater peace of mind for both businesses and consumers.

In addition to improving traceability and transparency, blockchain technology can also streamline supply chain operations by automating key processes such as payments and contract execution. Smart contracts, which are self-executing contracts with the terms of the agreement directly written into code, can be used to automatically trigger payments or actions when certain conditions are met. For example, a smart contract could be programmed to release payment to a supplier as soon as a shipment is verified as delivered, reducing the need for manual processing and speeding up transaction times. This level of automation enhances efficiency, reduces administrative overhead, and improves cash flow management for businesses.

Automation and robotics are also revolutionizing the landscape of supply chain management, particularly in the areas of warehousing and manufacturing. Automated warehouses, equipped with robotic systems and automated guided vehicles (AGVs), are enabling businesses to significantly increase efficiency by reducing the need for manual labor and minimizing human error. In these warehouses, robots can pick, pack, and move items with speed and precision, allowing companies to fulfill orders faster and more accurately. For example, e-commerce giants like Amazon have invested heavily in warehouse automation to enhance their order fulfillment processes, reducing the time it takes to process and ship products to customers.

In manufacturing, robotics and automation technologies, such as 3D printing, are enabling businesses to produce goods more efficiently and cost-effectively. 3D printing, in particular, has the potential to revolutionize supply chains by enabling companies to produce customized products on demand, reducing the need for large inventories and long lead times. For example, in the automotive industry, 3D printing can be used to produce specialized components or parts as needed, eliminating the need to stockpile large quantities of inventory. By decentralizing production and bringing it closer to the point of consumption, 3D printing also reduces transportation costs and emissions, contributing to more sustainable supply chains.

While technology offers significant benefits, its adoption is not without challenges. One of the primary challenges businesses face when implementing new technologies is the need for significant investment in infrastructure, systems, and training. Advanced technologies, such as AI, blockchain, and automation, often require large capital expenditures, making it difficult for small and medium-sized enterprises (SMEs) to compete with larger companies that have more resources to invest in cutting-edge solutions. Additionally, the integration of new technologies into existing supply chain systems can be complex and time-consuming, requiring careful planning, coordination, and change management to ensure a smooth transition.

Another major challenge associated with the adoption of technology in supply chain management is the growing concern over data security and privacy. As supply chains become more digitized and reliant on interconnected systems, they become more vulnerable to cyberattacks and data breaches. Hackers can target critical systems, such as inventory management software or transportation tracking platforms, potentially disrupting operations or stealing sensitive data. To mitigate these risks, businesses must invest in robust cybersecurity measures, including encryption, multi-factor authentication, and regular vulnerability assessments. Additionally, companies must ensure that their supply chain partners adhere to the same high standards of cybersecurity to prevent vulnerabilities from compromising the entire supply chain.

Despite these challenges, the benefits of leveraging technology in supply chain management far outweigh the risks. Companies that successfully adopt and integrate advanced technologies can gain a significant competitive advantage by improving efficiency, reducing costs, enhancing visibility, and delivering better customer experiences. In today's increasingly digital and fast-paced world, the ability to innovate and adapt through technology is essential for businesses that want to stay ahead of the competition and thrive in the global marketplace.

In conclusion, technology is revolutionizing supply chain management by providing businesses with new tools to optimize their operations and gain a competitive edge. From data analytics and predictive modeling to IoT, blockchain, and automation, these technologies are enabling companies to improve efficiency, enhance transparency, and build more resilient supply chains. However, businesses must carefully manage the challenges associated with technology adoption, including the need for significant investment and the risks of cybersecurity threats. By embracing innovation and leveraging the power of technology, companies can create supply chains that are not only efficient and cost-effective but also flexible, sustainable, and customer-focused, positioning themselves for long-term success in an increasingly complex and digital world.

Ndubueze Kelvin Anyamele

CHAPTER SEVEN
Building a Sustainable and Ethical Supply Chain

As the world grapples with environmental challenges such as climate change, resource depletion, and pollution, businesses are increasingly being called upon to adopt more sustainable and ethical practices in their supply chains. Consumers, governments, and investors are demanding greater transparency and accountability from companies, particularly in industries that have traditionally had a significant environmental and social impact, such as manufacturing, retail, and agriculture. In response, many businesses are rethinking their supply chain strategies to prioritize sustainability, reduce waste, and ensure that their operations are aligned with ethical and environmental standards.

In this chapter, we will explore the importance of building sustainable and ethical supply chains, the challenges involved in this transformation, and practical strategies that companies can implement to reduce their environmental footprint and enhance social responsibility. We will also examine how businesses can turn sustainability into a competitive advantage by meeting the demands of environmentally conscious consumers and staying ahead of regulatory requirements.

The concept of sustainability in supply chains encompasses a wide range of practices aimed at reducing the environmental and social impact of a company's operations. This includes minimizing resource consumption, reducing greenhouse gas emissions, promoting fair labor practices, and ensuring that suppliers meet ethical standards. In essence, a sustainable supply chain seeks to create value not only for the business but also for society and the environment.

One of the primary drivers of sustainability in supply chains is the growing awareness among consumers about the environmental and social impact of the products they purchase. Today's consumers are more informed than ever before, and many are willing to pay a premium for products that are produced sustainably and ethically. This shift in consumer behavior has prompted businesses to take a closer look at their supply chains and adopt more sustainable practices in order to meet the expectations of their customers.

At the same time, governments around the world are introducing stricter regulations aimed at reducing carbon emissions, promoting sustainable resource use, and ensuring fair labor practices. For example, the European Union's Green Deal aims to achieve net-zero carbon emissions by 2050, and many countries have implemented legislation requiring companies to disclose their environmental and social impact. Businesses that fail to comply with these regulations risk facing fines, legal action, and reputational damage.

One of the key challenges in building a sustainable supply chain is balancing sustainability with profitability. Many companies are concerned that adopting more sustainable practices will increase costs, particularly in industries where margins are already tight. For example, sourcing materials from suppliers that adhere to strict environmental and labor standards may be more expensive than sourcing from low-cost suppliers in regions with less stringent regulations.

Similarly, reducing carbon emissions may require investments in new technologies or more efficient transportation methods, which can increase operational costs.

However, while the upfront costs of implementing sustainable practices may be higher, businesses that prioritize sustainability can reap significant long-term benefits. For one, sustainability initiatives often lead to increased efficiency and cost savings over time. For example, reducing energy consumption in manufacturing facilities or switching to renewable energy sources can lower utility costs. Similarly, optimizing transportation routes to reduce fuel consumption can result in significant savings on logistics costs.

Moreover, companies that invest in sustainability are often better positioned to mitigate risks associated with supply chain disruptions. Climate change, for example, is already having a significant impact on global supply chains, with extreme weather events such as floods, droughts, and hurricanes disrupting the production and transportation of goods. By adopting more sustainable practices, such as diversifying suppliers or investing in climate-resilient infrastructure, businesses can reduce their vulnerability to these risks and ensure the continuity of their operations.

Transparency and traceability are essential components of a sustainable and ethical supply chain. Consumers and regulators are increasingly demanding that companies provide detailed information about the origin of their products, the environmental impact of their operations, and the working conditions of their employees and suppliers. This requires businesses to have full visibility into every stage of their supply chain, from raw material sourcing to manufacturing and distribution.

One of the most effective ways to achieve transparency and traceability in supply chains is through the use of technology. Blockchain, for example, can be used to create an immutable record of every transaction and movement of goods throughout the supply chain. This allows businesses to verify the authenticity and sustainability of their products and provide customers with detailed information about where their products come from and how they are produced. Similarly, IoT devices can be used to monitor environmental conditions throughout the supply chain, such as temperature and humidity levels, to ensure that products are transported in a way that minimizes waste and environmental impact.

In addition to adopting sustainable practices, businesses must also ensure that their supply chains are aligned with ethical standards. This includes ensuring that suppliers adhere to fair labor practices, such as paying workers a living wage, providing safe working conditions, and avoiding the use of child labor or forced labor. Many businesses implement supplier codes of conduct and conducting regular audits to ensure compliance with these standards.

Building a sustainable and ethical supply chain also requires collaboration with suppliers, customers, and other stakeholders. Businesses cannot achieve sustainability on their own because they must work together with their suppliers to develop more sustainable sourcing and production methods, as well as with customers to promote responsible consumption. For example, companies can collaborate with suppliers to reduce packaging waste by developing more sustainable packaging materials or working to eliminate single-use plastics. Similarly, businesses can encourage customers to make more sustainable choices by offering products that are certified as environmentally friendly or ethically produced.

While building a sustainable and ethical supply chain can be challenging, businesses that make this transformation can gain a significant competitive advantage. As consumers become more environmentally conscious, companies that prioritize sustainability are likely to see increased customer loyalty and brand value. Moreover, businesses that stay ahead of regulatory requirements can avoid the costs and risks associated with non-compliance, such as fines or reputational damage.

In conclusion, building a sustainable and ethical supply chain is not only a moral imperative but also a business opportunity. By adopting more sustainable practices, businesses can reduce their environmental footprint, enhance social responsibility, and meet the growing demands of consumers and regulators. Furthermore, sustainability can be a key driver of innovation, efficiency, and long-term success, allowing businesses to gain a competitive advantage in an increasingly conscious marketplace.

CHAPTER EIGHT
The Importance of Supplier Relationships in Competitive Supply Chains

In today's competitive landscape, where speed, efficiency, and innovation determine success, the strength of a company's supplier relationships can significantly influence its competitive advantage. Supplier relationships are no longer just transactional exchanges, where the primary goal is to secure the lowest possible price. Instead, businesses increasingly view their suppliers as strategic partners, vital to their supply chain's resilience, flexibility, and ability to innovate. The evolving nature of global supply chains, the pressure to reduce lead times, and the growing complexity of product design have shifted the focus to cultivating long-term, collaborative relationships with suppliers.

The importance of strong supplier relationships cannot be overstated. These relationships allow businesses to foster trust and collaboration, enabling both parties to share knowledge, co-create value, and solve problems more effectively. By working closely with suppliers, companies can achieve greater efficiencies, reduce costs, and improve product quality. Moreover, close relationships allow businesses to respond more rapidly to shifts in demand, changes in market conditions, or unforeseen disruptions, something that has become increasingly crucial in today's volatile global environment.

One of the main benefits of cultivating strong supplier relationships is the ability to maintain high levels of trust. Trust is the cornerstone of any successful partnership, and it allows businesses and suppliers to communicate openly and honestly. When there is trust, suppliers are more likely to be transparent about potential issues, such as delays, capacity constraints, or quality concerns, which allows businesses to take proactive measures to mitigate risks. Similarly, businesses are more likely to share critical information with their suppliers, such as forecasts, long-term plans, and market intelligence, which helps suppliers align their operations with the business's strategic objectives.

This level of transparency leads to more effective problem-solving. When both parties work collaboratively, they can identify bottlenecks, inefficiencies, or other challenges in the supply chain and develop joint solutions. This can range from finding ways to streamline production processes, reducing lead times, or improving the quality of raw materials. In many cases, suppliers bring their own expertise and insights to the table, offering innovative solutions that the company may not have considered. This collaborative approach not only enhances operational efficiency but also fosters a culture of continuous improvement within the supply chain.

In addition to improving operational efficiency, strong supplier relationships also contribute to greater supply chain flexibility. In an increasingly uncertain global market, where disruptions caused by geopolitical events, natural disasters, or economic shifts are becoming more frequent, flexibility is essential. Businesses that maintain close relationships with their suppliers are better positioned to respond to these disruptions. For example, if a key supplier is unable to deliver materials due to a natural disaster, a company with strong supplier relationships may be able to quickly source materials from an alternate supplier within its network. Suppliers are also more likely to prioritize their most trusted partners when resources are limited, helping companies avoid costly delays.

Beyond flexibility, close supplier relationships are key to driving innovation. Suppliers often have valuable insights into new materials, technologies, or processes that can enhance the company's product offerings. By working together, businesses and suppliers can co-develop new products or improve existing ones, creating a competitive advantage in the market. For example, a supplier with expertise in sustainable materials may help a company reduce its environmental impact by introducing eco-friendly alternatives that meet or exceed current performance standards. This type of collaboration can lead to innovations that differentiate the company from its competitors, improve customer satisfaction, and open up new market opportunities.

However, building strong supplier relationships requires time, effort, and a shift in mindset. Instead of viewing suppliers solely as cost centers, businesses must treat them as strategic partners who can contribute to their long-term success. This means going beyond simply negotiating for the best price and instead focusing on value creation, trust-building, and mutual growth. To achieve this, companies need to invest in developing these relationships by regularly engaging with suppliers, understanding their capabilities and challenges, and ensuring that both parties are aligned to shared goals.

One of the ways businesses can build stronger supplier relationships is by creating clear performance expectations and metrics. By setting key performance indicators (KPIs) related to quality, delivery times, innovation, and sustainability, companies can provide suppliers with a clear understanding of what is expected and measure their performance objectively. Regular performance reviews allow businesses and suppliers to discuss areas for improvement and celebrate successes, strengthening the relationship over time.

Another important aspect of supplier relationship management is collaboration in risk management. In an interconnected global supply chain, risks such as supply disruptions, quality issues, or regulatory changes can have far-reaching consequences. Businesses that work closely with their suppliers to identify and mitigate risks can build more resilient supply chains. For instance, businesses can collaborate with suppliers to diversify sourcing locations, build inventory buffers, or invest in technology that enhances supply chain visibility. These strategies not only protect the business from potential disruptions but also demonstrate a commitment to the long-term success of the supplier, further deepening the partnership.

Supplier relationships also play a critical role in ensuring sustainability and ethical practices within the supply chain. As consumers, investors, and regulators increasingly demand transparency and accountability in how products are sourced and produced, businesses are under pressure to ensure that their suppliers meet environmental and social standards. Close relationships with suppliers enable businesses to work together to achieve sustainability goals, such as reducing carbon emissions, minimizing waste, and ensuring fair labor practices. In many cases, suppliers are willing to collaborate on sustainability initiatives that benefit both parties, such as developing more energy-efficient manufacturing processes or using recycled materials.

A successful example of the importance of strong supplier relationships can be seen in industries such as automotive and electronics, where complex products require a high degree of collaboration between manufacturers and suppliers. In these industries, businesses often rely on a network of tier-one and tier-two suppliers to provide critical components. By fostering long-term relationships with these suppliers, companies are able to ensure a steady supply of high-quality components, reduce lead times, and drive innovation in areas such as lightweight materials, advanced electronics, and fuel-efficient technologies. These relationships are built on mutual trust, continuous communication, and a shared commitment to quality and innovation.

As businesses continue to expand globally and supply chains grow more complex, the importance of supplier relationships will only increase. Companies that prioritize supplier relationships as a key component of their supply chain strategy will be better positioned to navigate the challenges of a dynamic global market, adapt to changing customer demands, and stay ahead of their competitors. In contrast, businesses that neglect their supplier relationships risk facing supply chain disruptions, higher costs, and missed opportunities for innovation.

In conclusion, supplier relationships are a critical driver of competitive advantage in modern supply chains. By moving beyond transactional interactions and cultivating long-term, collaborative partnerships with suppliers, businesses can unlock significant benefits in terms of efficiency, flexibility, innovation, and risk management. Strong supplier relationships not only enhance operational performance but also create opportunities for co-innovation and shared value creation, positioning businesses for long-term success in an increasingly complex and competitive global marketplace.

Ndubueze Kelvin Anyamele

CHAPTER NINE
Sourcing and Procurement Strategies for Competitive Advantage

Sourcing and procurement lie at the heart of supply chain management, and the way businesses manage these functions can significantly affect their overall competitiveness. Companies today operate in an environment where the efficient acquisition of goods and services is critical not only to cost control but also to maintaining product quality, innovation, and responsiveness to market changes. The strategies businesses employ in sourcing and procurement determine how well they can meet these objectives, and by extension, how well they can compete in their industries.

Effective sourcing and procurement strategies go beyond simple cost-cutting. While reducing costs remains an essential goal, businesses must also consider other factors such as supplier reliability, product quality, lead times, and risk mitigation. A procurement strategy that focuses solely on price often leads to vulnerabilities, including supply chain disruptions, poor product quality, or difficulties in responding to changing market conditions. As a result, modern companies increasingly focus on optimizing procurement through strategic supplier relationships, risk management, and technology integration, all while aligning procurement goals with broader business objectives.

Sourcing refers to the process of identifying and selecting suppliers that provide the materials, components, or services required for production. Procurement involves acquiring those goods or services and managing relationships with suppliers. Together, these functions play a critical role in ensuring that a business has access to the resources it needs, at the right quantity, at the right time, and at the right price. But sourcing and procurement are about much more than just ensuring the flow of goods they are about creating value throughout the supply chain.

Global sourcing has become a dominant trend in procurement strategy, allowing businesses to access suppliers across different geographies and tap into lower-cost regions. By sourcing globally, companies can reduce their costs by taking advantage of lower labor rates, raw material availability, or favorable exchange rates. For instance, many electronics manufacturers source components from Asia, where skilled labor is available at a lower cost than in other parts of the world. However, global sourcing also introduces new challenges, including managing longer lead times, navigating complex customs regulations, and dealing with the risks of geopolitical instability.

One key aspect of effective sourcing is supplier diversification. Relying too heavily on a single supplier or a single region for critical materials can expose a company to significant risk. If a supplier experiences operational issues, or if a region is affected by natural disasters or political instability, the business could face delays, shortages, or increased costs. Diversifying the supplier base reduces this risk by ensuring that the company has multiple options for sourcing critical materials. For example, a company that sources raw materials from both Asia and South America will be better positioned to handle a disruption in one region by shifting its procurement to another.

Strategic procurement also requires companies to evaluate suppliers based on criteria beyond cost. Quality, reliability, and the capacity to meet changing demand are all essential factors. A supplier that offers the lowest price but frequently misses delivery deadlines or provides inconsistent quality will ultimately cost the business more in lost sales, production delays, and damage to its reputation. On the other hand, a supplier that consistently delivers high-quality products on time, even at a slightly higher price, can help the business improve customer satisfaction, reduce waste, and avoid costly rework.

To build strong supplier relationships, businesses need to focus on collaboration and communication. Suppliers that understand a company's long-term needs and strategic goals are better positioned to provide the right level of service. Open communication helps both parties align their expectations and work together to solve problems as they arise. This can include joint planning efforts, where companies share forecasts with suppliers, allowing them to plan their production schedules more effectively and avoid capacity constraints. It may also involve sharing technology and process improvements, such as implementing joint quality control measures or introducing more sustainable manufacturing practices.

Sustainability has become a critical consideration in sourcing and procurement strategies. As consumer awareness of environmental issues grows, businesses are under increasing pressure to ensure that their suppliers adhere to ethical and sustainable practices. Companies that fail to do so risk damaging their reputation and alienating environmentally conscious customers. Many companies now include sustainability criteria when evaluating suppliers, favoring those that have strong environmental credentials, such as reducing carbon emissions, using recycled materials, or supporting fair labor practices. This emphasis on sustainability not only helps businesses meet regulatory requirements but also positions them as leaders in the growing market for green products.

Technology plays a vital role in optimizing sourcing and procurement processes. Digital procurement platforms allow companies to automate many of the routine tasks associated with procurement, such as placing orders, tracking shipments, and managing invoices. By using procurement software, companies can gain real-time visibility into their supply chain, allowing them to monitor supplier performance, identify potential bottlenecks, and make data-driven decisions to improve efficiency. Additionally, technologies like blockchain are being used to improve transparency in supply chains by providing a secure and immutable record of every transaction and shipment, making it easier to trace the origin of materials and verify compliance with ethical standards.

In the context of global sourcing, businesses must also navigate the complexities of international trade regulations, tariffs, and logistics. Managing customs compliance and ensuring that shipments move smoothly across borders requires a deep understanding of the regulatory environment in each country where the business operates. Companies that source materials from multiple countries must also account for differences in labor laws, environmental regulations, and trade agreements, all of which can affect the cost and availability of goods. This makes it essential for businesses to work closely with logistics providers, customs brokers, and legal advisors to ensure that their sourcing strategy is compliant and cost-effective.

In addition to managing the day-to-day operations of sourcing and procurement, businesses must also focus on long-term risk management. Supply chain disruptions, whether caused by natural disasters, pandemics, political instability, or economic crises, can have far-reaching effects on procurement. As a result, businesses need to develop contingency plans that allow them to continue sourcing critical materials in the event of a disruption. This might involve maintaining safety stock levels, diversifying suppliers, or investing in alternative materials. For example, during the COVID-19 pandemic, many businesses experienced disruptions in their global supply chains due to factory shutdowns and transportation delays. Companies that had diversified their supplier base or built strong relationships with multiple suppliers were better able to navigate these challenges and maintain their operations.

Another critical component of procurement strategy is cost management. While businesses must be cautious not to prioritize cost over quality or reliability, finding ways to reduce procurement costs without compromising performance remains a key objective. This can be achieved through volume discounts, negotiating long-term contracts with suppliers, or leveraging economies of scale. Companies can also reduce costs by working with suppliers to streamline production processes, eliminate waste, or improve efficiency. For example, a manufacturer might work with a supplier to redesign packaging in a way that reduces shipping costs or optimizes the use of warehouse space.

Strategic sourcing decisions also need to consider the company's future growth and innovation goals. Suppliers should not only meet the company's current needs but also have the capacity to scale as the business grows or to support new product development. In many industries, such as electronics or automotive, suppliers play a crucial role in innovation by introducing new technologies, materials, or processes. Companies that build strong relationships with innovative suppliers can gain access to cutting-edge solutions that enhance their product offerings and differentiate them from competitors.

Ultimately, the success of sourcing and procurement strategies depends on how well these activities are aligned with the company's broader business objectives. Procurement teams need to work closely with other departments, such as product development, manufacturing, and marketing, to ensure that sourcing decisions support the company's goals for growth, quality, and customer satisfaction. For example, if a company's goal is to launch a new product that meets high sustainability standards, the procurement team will need to identify suppliers that can provide environmentally friendly materials while still meeting cost and quality targets.

In conclusion, sourcing and procurement are critical functions that directly impact a company's ability to compete in the marketplace. By adopting strategic sourcing models, diversifying suppliers, prioritizing quality and reliability, and leveraging technology, businesses can optimize their procurement processes and create a more resilient and flexible supply chain. Moreover, by focusing on sustainability and ethical sourcing, companies can not only meet regulatory requirements but also appeal to the growing market of environmentally conscious consumers. In today's global economy, where supply chain disruptions are becoming more frequent, businesses that develop robust sourcing and procurement strategies will be better positioned to maintain continuity, drive innovation, and achieve long-term success.

CHAPTER TEN
Global Logistics and Distribution: Overcoming Challenges

Logistics and distribution are the lifeblood of global supply chains. These functions ensure that raw materials, components, and finished products are more efficiently from one point to another, crossing borders, time zones, and often multiple regulatory frameworks. As businesses expand their operations globally, the complexity of managing logistics increases. It is no longer just about moving goods from one place to another; it's about doing so in a way that maximizes efficiency, minimizes costs, and ensures timely delivery while navigating a complex web of challenges.

For a company to maintain a competitive edge, its logistics and distribution strategies must be finely tuned. A business that can move goods faster and more efficiently than its competitors will have a significant advantage, especially in industries where speed to market is critical. At the same time, logistical efficiency translates directly into cost savings, helping businesses maintain profitability in highly competitive environments. However, achieving logistical excellence on a global scale requires overcoming a host of challenges, from transportation delays and fluctuating fuel prices to customs regulations and environmental concerns.

One of the most significant challenges in global logistics is managing transportation across multiple modes, including air, sea, rail, and road. Each mode of transport has its advantages and limitations, and choosing the right one can make a substantial difference in both cost and delivery times. Air transport, for example, is the fastest option but also the most expensive, making it suitable for high-value, time-sensitive goods. Sea freight, on the other hand, is more economical for bulk shipments but involves longer lead times. The key for businesses is to optimize their use of different transportation modes based on the nature of the product, the urgency of the shipment, and the cost considerations.

For many companies, balancing these modes in a cost-effective way while meeting customer expectations for timely delivery is a constant challenge. Some businesses employ multi-modal strategies, where goods move across different transportation modes in a single journey to achieve both speed and cost-efficiency. For example, a company might use air freight for the initial leg of a journey to meet a tight deadline and then switch to rail or road transport for the final delivery to reduce costs.

Another challenge is the increasing complexity of cross-border logistics. As companies move goods across international boundaries, they must navigate a host of customs regulations, trade agreements, and tariffs, all of which can vary significantly from one country to the next. Customs procedures, in particular, can cause delays if documentation is incomplete or if goods are subject to inspection. In some regions, customs clearance can take days or even weeks, disrupting supply chain timelines and increasing costs.

To overcome these challenges, many businesses invest in technology solutions that automate customs documentation and provide real-time tracking of shipments. Trade management software, for example, helps companies ensure compliance with international trade laws, calculate tariffs, and generate the necessary paperwork to expedite customs clearance. These technologies reduce the risk of delays and help companies avoid costly penalties or fines for non-compliance with customs regulations.

Inventory management is another critical aspect of global logistics. Companies must carefully manage their inventory levels to avoid stockouts, which can lead to missed sales, or overstocking, which ties up valuable capital in unsold goods. Global distribution adds complexity to inventory management, as businesses must account for longer lead times, fluctuating demand in different markets, and potential disruptions in transportation.

One strategy for optimizing inventory management in global logistics is to implement just-in-time (JIT) systems, where materials and products are delivered precisely when they are needed for production or sale. JIT systems minimize the amount of inventory that businesses need to hold, reducing storage costs and freeing up capital. However, this approach also requires a highly reliable logistics network, as any delays in delivery can disrupt production or sales.

To mitigate the risks associated with JIT inventory management, companies can use technology to improve visibility in their supply chains. Real-time tracking systems, for example, allow businesses to monitor the status of shipments as they move through the supply chain, providing early warnings of potential delays. This enables companies to make quick adjustments, such as rerouting shipments or adjusting inventory levels in other locations, to avoid disruptions.

Warehousing and distribution centers are also critical components of global logistics. As businesses expand their global operations, they often need to establish distribution centers in key regions to ensure timely delivery of goods to customers. These distribution centers act as hubs where goods are received, stored, and shipped to their final destinations. The location and efficiency of these centers can have a significant impact on a company's ability to meet customer demands and control costs.

Choosing the right location for distribution centers is a strategic decision that requires careful analysis of factors such as proximity to key markets, transportation infrastructure, and labor costs. For example, a company that serves European markets might choose to locate its distribution center in a country with excellent transportation links, such as the Netherlands, which has one of the most efficient logistics infrastructures in the region. Once the distribution center is operational, companies must invest in warehouse management systems (WMS) to optimize the flow of goods in and out of the facility, minimize handling times, and reduce storage costs.

The rise of e-commerce has also transformed global logistics and distribution. Consumers now expect fast, reliable shipping, often at low or no cost, regardless of where they are located. This has created enormous pressure on logistics networks to handle a growing volume of small, individual orders while still maintaining efficiency and controlling costs. E-commerce companies, in particular, must navigate the challenge of "last mile" delivery the final leg of the delivery process, which brings goods directly to the customer's door. The last mile is often the most expensive and inefficient part of the logistics chain, especially in urban areas where traffic congestion or inadequate infrastructure can cause delays.

To address the challenges of last-mile delivery, some companies are experimenting with innovative solutions such as drone deliveries, autonomous vehicles, and local fulfillment centers. These technologies have the potential to reduce delivery times and costs while providing greater flexibility in meeting customer demands. For example, local fulfillment centers located near major cities allow companies to store inventory closer to customers, reducing the time and cost associated with delivering goods from distant warehouses.

Another growing trend in global logistics is the push toward sustainability. As consumers become more environmentally conscious, businesses are under increasing pressure to reduce the environmental impact of their logistics operations. Transportation is a major contributor to greenhouse gas emissions, and companies that rely heavily on long-haul shipping or air freight may face scrutiny for their carbon footprints. To address this issue, many businesses are investing in greener logistics solutions, such as using electric vehicles for deliveries, optimizing transportation routes to reduce fuel consumption, and partnering with logistics providers that prioritize sustainability.

Some companies are also exploring the use of alternative fuels, such as biofuels or hydrogen, to power their fleets. Additionally, the concept of carbon-neutral shipping is gaining traction, where companies offset their carbon emissions by investing in environmental projects such as reforestation or renewable energy. These initiatives not only help businesses reduce their environmental impact but also appeal to consumers who are increasingly making purchasing decisions based on a company's sustainability practices.

Risk management is another crucial component of global logistics. Supply chain disruptions, whether caused by natural disasters, political instability, or global pandemics, can have devastating effects on a company's ability to move goods.

The COVID-19 pandemic, for example, exposed the vulnerabilities of global supply chains as factories shut down, transportation networks were disrupted, and borders were closed. Companies that lacked resilience in their logistics networks faced significant challenges in maintaining operations.

To build more resilient logistics networks, businesses are increasingly focusing on diversifying their supply chains, investing in technology to improve visibility, and developing contingency plans for potential disruptions. Diversification might involve sourcing materials from multiple suppliers in different regions, reducing dependence on a single transportation route, or holding strategic reserves of critical materials in case of supply shortages. Technology, such as predictive analytics and real-time monitoring systems, allows businesses to anticipate disruptions and respond quickly, minimizing the impact on their operations.

Finally, global logistics and distribution are heavily influenced by changing regulatory environments. Trade policies, tariffs, and customs regulations can shift rapidly, affecting the cost and speed of moving goods across borders. Businesses must stay up to date with these changes and be prepared to adjust their logistics strategies accordingly. For example, the imposition of new tariffs between the United States and China in recent years forced many companies to reconfigure their supply chains, sourcing goods from different countries or adjusting their pricing to account for the increased costs.

In conclusion, global logistics and distribution are critical functions that enable businesses to compete in an increasingly interconnected world. However, the challenges of managing transportation across borders, optimizing inventory levels, handling last-mile deliveries, and addressing sustainability concerns require companies to adopt innovative strategies and invest in technology. By overcoming these challenges and building resilient, efficient logistics networks, businesses can improve their speed to market, control costs, and enhance customer satisfaction, all of which contribute to long-term competitive advantage.

CHAPTER ELEVEN
Customer-Centric Supply Chains for Competitive Differentiation

In today's marketplace, customer expectations are higher than ever. The rise of e-commerce, the acceleration of technology, and the global nature of competition have all contributed to a shift in consumer behavior, where fast delivery, product availability, and personalized experiences are no longer just desired they are expected. In response to this, businesses are increasingly focusing on building customer-centric supply chains that place the needs and preferences of their customers at the forefront of their operational strategies.

A customer-centric supply chain is designed to be flexible, responsive, and focused on delivering exceptional service at every touchpoint. This approach goes beyond simply meeting customer demands; it seeks to exceed expectations by creating supply chains that are agile enough to adapt quickly to changes in demand, offer high levels of customization, and provide real-time visibility and communication. The ability to consistently deliver value to customers through a highly efficient and responsive supply chain is a key source of competitive differentiation in many industries.

One of the central tenets of a customer-centric supply chain is flexibility. Traditional supply chains were designed to maximize efficiency, often at the expense of flexibility. They were optimized for large, standardized production runs and operated on long lead times to minimize costs. However, in today's fast-paced market, where consumer preferences can shift rapidly, businesses must be able to pivot quickly to respond to changing demand patterns. A rigid, inflexible supply chain risks being left behind, unable to keep up with the speed of the market.

Flexibility in the supply chain enables businesses to offer more customization to their customers, which has become a critical differentiator in many industries. Consumers today expect products that are tailored to their individual preferences, whether it's personalized apparel, custom-built electronics, or unique service experiences. A customer-centric supply chain is capable of delivering these customized offerings by incorporating technologies like modular manufacturing, just-in-time production, and advanced data analytics to forecast demand and adjust production schedules accordingly.

Agility is another important characteristic of a customer-centric supply chain. Agility refers to the ability to respond quickly to changes in demand, supply disruptions, or other market fluctuations. Agile supply chains are built on the principle of responsiveness, where businesses can adjust their operations in real time to meet customer needs. This might involve accelerating production in response to a sudden surge in demand, rerouting shipments to avoid delays, or scaling down operations in anticipation of slower sales. An agile supply chain requires close collaboration with suppliers, real-time visibility into inventory levels and transportation status, and the ability to make data-driven decisions quickly.

In addition to flexibility and agility, customer-centric supply chains are increasingly focused on improving transparency and communication. Customers today expect to be kept informed about the status of their orders; from the moment they place an order to the moment it arrives at their doorstep. Real-time visibility in the supply chain is essential for meeting these expectations. By providing customers with accurate, up-to-date information about their orders, businesses can enhance the customer experience and build trust.

Technology plays a critical role in enabling transparency and communication in the supply chain. Many businesses are leveraging digital platforms and tools to provide customers with real-time updates on the status of their orders, including tracking information, estimated delivery times, and notifications of any delays or changes. These tools not only improve the customer experience but also allow businesses to identify potential issues in the supply chain and take corrective action before they impact customer satisfaction.

To create a truly customer-centric supply chain, businesses must also embrace data-driven decision-making. The vast amount of data generated by supply chain operations, customer interactions, and market trends provides businesses with valuable insights into customer preferences, buying behaviors, and demand patterns. By analyzing this data, businesses can better understand what their customers want and adjust their supply chain strategies to meet those needs. For example, by analyzing past sales data, a retailer can forecast demand for specific products during peak seasons and adjust its inventory levels to ensure that popular items are always in stock.

Data analytics can also help businesses identify opportunities for improving the customer experience. For instance, a company might analyze data on delivery times to identify bottlenecks in its logistics network and implement changes to improve speed and reliability. Similarly, businesses can use data to personalize the customer experience by offering tailored recommendations based on a customer's previous purchases or browsing history.

While technology and data analytics are important enablers of customer-centric supply chains, the human element should not be overlooked. Customer service remains a critical touchpoint in the supply chain, particularly when things go wrong. Businesses that prioritize customer service and ensure that their supply chain teams are responsive, knowledgeable, and empowered to resolve issues quickly will create a better overall experience for their customers. This, in turn, can lead to greater customer loyalty and repeat business, both of which are key to long-term success.

Sustainability is another growing concern for customers, and businesses with customer-centric supply chains are increasingly focusing on creating more sustainable operations. Consumers are becoming more aware of the environmental impact of the products they buy and the companies they support. As a result, they expect businesses to take responsibility for minimizing the environmental footprint of their supply chains. Companies that prioritize sustainability by reducing carbon emissions, minimizing waste, and sourcing materials responsibly not only meet customer expectations but also create a competitive advantage in the market.

To build a customer-centric supply chain, businesses must foster close relationships with their suppliers. Suppliers play a critical role in ensuring g that products are delivered on time, meet quality standards, and are available in the quantities needed to satisfy customer demand. By working closely with suppliers, businesses can improve collaboration, share real-time information, and co-develop solutions that enhance customer satisfaction. Strong supplier relationships also enable businesses to be more agile and responsive, as they can rely on their suppliers to meet changing requirements or overcome disruptions quickly.

In conclusion, customer-centric supply chains are essential for businesses that want to differentiate themselves in today's competitive market. By prioritizing flexibility, agility, transparency, and data-driven decision-making, companies can create supply chains that are not only efficient but also responsive to the evolving needs and expectations of their customers. Whether through improved delivery times, personalized products, or enhanced communication, a customer-centric supply chain can help businesses build stronger relationships with their customers, increase customer satisfaction, and drive long-term growth.

CHAPTER TWELVE
Data-Driven Decision Making in Supply Chain Management

In the age of digital transformation, data has emerged as one of the most powerful tools for optimizing supply chain management. The ability to collect, analyze, and act upon vast amounts of data allows companies to improve every aspect of their supply chains from forecasting demand and managing inventory to optimizing transportation and improving supplier performance. Data-driven decision making enables companies to respond more quickly to market changes, reduce operational inefficiencies, and make informed strategic choices that drive competitive advantage.

Supply chains, by their nature, generate enormous quantities of data at every stage of the process. From the sourcing of raw materials and components to manufacturing, distribution, and final delivery, every movement, transaction, and interaction produces data that can be captured and analyzed. However, until recently, much of this data was siloed, inaccessible, or underutilized, with companies relying on manual processes and fragmented systems to make critical decisions. This often led to inefficiencies, misaligned inventories, and delays in responding to demand fluctuations.

Today, advances in data analytics, machine learning, and artificial intelligence (AI) have revolutionized supply chain management. By leveraging these technologies, businesses can harness the power of data to gain real-time visibility into their operations, predict future trends, and make faster, more accurate decisions. In this chapter, we will explore how data-driven decision making is transforming supply chains, the tools and technologies enabling this shift, and how companies can implement data analytics to improve performance and maintain a competitive edge.

One of the most impactful applications of data-driven decision making in supply chain management is demand forecasting. Accurate demand forecasts are critical for ensuring that businesses have the right amount of inventory to meet customer needs without overstocking, which ties up capital, or understocking, which leads to missed sales. Traditionally, demand forecasting relied on historical sales data and intuition, which often resulted in inaccurate predictions, especially in volatile or rapidly changing markets.

With the rise of big data and predictive analytics, businesses can now generate much more accurate demand forecasts by analyzing a wide range of factors that influence consumer behavior. These might include historical sales patterns, market trends, weather conditions, economic indicators, and even social media sentiment. By feeding this data into machine learning algorithms, companies can uncover patterns and correlations that would be impossible to detect manually, allowing them to predict demand with greater precision.

For example, a retailer might use data analytics to forecast demand for winter coats based not only on last year's sales but also on real-time weather data, fashion trends, and consumer sentiment on social media. This enables the company to adjust its procurement and production schedules in advance, ensuring that it has enough inventory to meet demand while avoiding the costs associated with overproduction.

Inventory management is another area where data-driven decision making can significantly improve efficiency. Managing inventory levels is a delicate balancing act. Too much inventory can lead to high holding costs, while too little can result in stockouts and lost sales. Data analytics allows companies to optimize their inventory by providing real-time visibility into stock levels, lead times, and demand forecasts. By using predictive analytics, businesses can anticipate when they will need to reorder stock, how much inventory they should hold, and where that inventory should be located to best meet customer demand.

Advanced data analytics tools, such as demand sensing and real-time inventory tracking, provide a granular view of inventory across the entire supply chain. This enables businesses to dynamically adjust their inventory levels based on actual demand, production schedules, and market conditions. Companies that implement real-time inventory tracking systems can reduce lead times, minimize excess stock, and avoid costly rush shipments or last-minute sourcing from unreliable suppliers.

Beyond forecasting and inventory management, data analytics also plays a critical role in optimizing transportation and logistics. Supply chain networks often span multiple continents, involving various transportation modes, warehouses, and distribution centers. Coordinating the movement of goods through these networks efficiently is essential for reducing transportation costs, improving delivery times, and minimizing environmental impact. By analyzing data on transportation routes, fuel costs, delivery times, and shipment volumes, businesses can identify opportunities to optimize their logistics operations.

For example, route optimization algorithms can analyze traffic patterns, weather conditions, and fuel prices to determine the most efficient delivery routes, reducing both costs and carbon emissions. Similarly, predictive maintenance analytics can help companies monitor the condition of their transportation fleets and identify potential mechanical issues before they result in costly breakdowns or delays. These data-driven insights enable companies to maintain smoother, more reliable logistics operations while reducing operational costs.

Supplier performance management is another critical aspect of supply chain optimization that benefits from data-driven decision making. Suppliers are essential partners in the supply chain, and their performance directly impacts a company's ability to meet production targets and deliver products to customers on time. Data analytics allows companies to continuously monitor supplier performance by tracking key metrics such as delivery reliability, lead times, quality levels, and cost competitiveness.

By analyzing these performance indicators, businesses can identify high-performing suppliers who consistently meet expectations, as well as underperforming suppliers who may be introducing inefficiencies or risks into the supply chain. In cases where supplier performance falls short, data analytics can help pinpoint the root causes of the issues, whether they are related to production capacity, logistics bottlenecks, or quality control problems. With this information, businesses can work collaboratively with suppliers to address these challenges, negotiate better terms, or, if necessary, switch to alternative suppliers who can better meet their requirements.

The rise of the Internet of Things (IoT) has further enhanced data-driven decision making in supply chain management by providing real-time, granular visibility into every stage of the supply chain. IoT devices, such as sensors and

RFID tags, can be used to track the movement of goods through warehouses, transportation networks, and retail locations. These devices generate a continuous stream of data that can be analyzed to provide insights into asset utilization, product condition, and the efficiency of various supply chain processes.

For example, IoT sensors can monitor the temperature and humidity levels of perishable goods in transit, ensuring that they are stored in optimal conditions to avoid spoilage. If any deviations are detected, the system can automatically alert logistics managers, who can take corrective action to prevent product loss. Similarly, RFID tags can be used to track inventory levels in real time, allowing businesses to gain a complete view of their stock levels across multiple locations and make data-driven decisions about replenishment, distribution, and fulfillment.

Data analytics is also transforming the way businesses manage supply chain risks. In a globalized world, supply chains are exposed to a wide range of risks, including natural disasters, political instability, economic volatility, and supply disruptions. Data-driven risk management systems enable companies to identify and mitigate these risks by analyzing both internal and external data sources. Predictive analytics can be used to assess the likelihood of disruptions, such as supplier bankruptcies, port closures, or transportation delays, and model their potential impact on the supply chain.

By using data to identify vulnerabilities in advance, businesses can develop contingency plans and take proactive measures to minimize the impact of disruptions. For example, a company might identify that one of its key suppliers is located in a region prone to natural disasters, such as hurricanes or earthquakes. Armed with this knowledge, the company can work with alternative suppliers to establish backup sourcing arrangements or hold safety stock to ensure that production can continue uninterrupted in the event of a disruption.

While the benefits of data-driven decision making in supply chain management are clear, implementing a successful data analytics strategy requires the right technology, processes, and organizational culture. One of the key challenges is integrating data from different sources across the supply chain, which may include suppliers, manufacturers, logistics providers, and customers. Many companies still rely on legacy systems that do not communicate with one another, making it difficult to gain a holistic view of the supply chain.

To overcome this challenge, businesses need to invest in integrated supply chain management platforms that can collect and analyze data from multiple sources in real time. These platforms often leverage cloud-based technology, enabling businesses to scale their data analytics capabilities as their supply chain networks grow. Additionally, companies need to ensure that their employees are equipped with the skills and knowledge to interpret data and make informed decisions. This may involve providing training on data analytics tools and fostering a culture of data-driven decision making within the organization.

Data privacy and security are also critical considerations when implementing data-driven decision making in supply chains. As supply chains become more digitized and interconnected, the risk of cyberattacks and data breaches increases. Companies must ensure that they have robust cybersecurity measures in place to protect sensitive data and prevent unauthorized access. This includes encrypting data, implementing multi-factor authentication, and regularly auditing supply chain systems for vulnerabilities.

In conclusion, data-driven decision making is revolutionizing supply chain management by enabling businesses to optimize their operations, reduce costs, and improve responsiveness to market changes. From demand forecasting and inventory management to logistics optimization and supplier performance monitoring, data analytics provides the insights companies need to make smarter, faster, and more accurate decisions. However, to fully realize the benefits of data-driven decision making, businesses must invest in the right technologies, processes, and skills, while ensuring that they protect their data from security threats. In an increasingly complex and competitive global market, the ability to harness the power of data will be a key differentiator for businesses looking to build agile, efficient, and resilient supply chains.

CHAPTER THIRTEEN
The Role of Culture and Leadership in Supply Chain Success

In the complex world of global supply chain management, culture and leadership play a critical role in determining success. While many companies focus on the technical aspects of optimizing their supply chains such as implementing new technologies, improving logistics, and streamlining procurement processes organizational culture and leadership are often overlooked. Yet, these "softer" factors are just as important as the technical ones in ensuring that supply chain operations are efficient, adaptable, and aligned with business goals.

A strong organizational culture fosters collaboration, innovation, and a sense of ownership among employees, which is essential for maintaining a high-performance supply chain. Meanwhile, effective leadership ensures that the supply chain strategy is clearly defined, communicated, and aligned with the overall business objectives. Leaders who understand the importance of supply chain management and empower their teams to make decisions can significantly enhance the company's ability to compete in the global market.

Culture is the set of shared values, beliefs, and behaviors that shape how people within an organization interact and work together. In the context of supply chain management, culture determines how employees approach problem-solving, collaborate with external partners, and respond to challenges. A culture that encourages open communication, innovation, and continuous improvement can lead to more agile and responsive supply chain operations, where teams proactively identify and solve problems before they escalate.

For example, a company with a strong culture of innovation is more likely to encourage its supply chain teams to explore new technologies, experiment with process improvements, and seek out ways to enhance efficiency. This culture empowers employees at all levels to contribute ideas and take initiative, rather than simply following established procedures. As a result, the supply chain becomes more dynamic, capable of adapting to changes in the market, and better equipped to handle disruptions.

On the other hand, a company with a rigid or hierarchical culture may stifle innovation and slow down decision-making. In such organizations, supply chain teams may be reluctant to suggest new approaches or challenge the status quo, even when they recognize inefficiencies. This can lead to a reactive, rather than proactive, approach to supply chain management, where problems are only addressed after they have caused significant delays or increased costs.

Building a culture that supports supply chain success requires a deliberate effort from leadership. Leaders must communicate the importance of the supply chain to the company's overall strategy and create an environment where employees feel empowered to take ownership of supply chain performance. This involves providing employees with the resources, training, and tools they need to succeed, as well as recognizing and rewarding their contributions to supply chain improvements.

Leadership is also critical in shaping the vision and strategy for the supply chain. Effective leaders are able to see the bigger picture, understanding how the supply chain fits into the company's long-term goals and how it can be leveraged to create a competitive advantage. They communicate this vision clearly to their teams, ensuring that everyone is aligned and working toward the same objectives. This alignment is essential for ensuring that supply chain decisions are made with the company's strategic priorities in mind.

Leaders who are actively engaged in supply chain management also foster a culture of accountability. By setting clear expectations and performance metrics, they ensure that teams are held responsible for delivering results. This accountability encourages employees to take ownership of their work and continuously seek ways to improve supply chain performance, whether by reducing costs, improving delivery times, or enhancing product quality.

Another important aspect of leadership in supply chain management is the ability to build and maintain strong relationships with external partners, such as suppliers, logistics providers, and customers. Successful supply chains rely on collaboration across multiple organizations, and leaders play a key role in facilitating these partnerships. By fostering trust, open communication, and mutual respect with external partners, leaders can create more resilient and flexible supply chains that are better able to respond to changing market conditions or disruptions.

Leadership also plays a crucial role in managing supply chain risks. In today's globalized world, supply chains are exposed to a wide range of risks, from natural disasters and political instability to economic volatility and cyberattacks. Effective leaders understand the importance of risk management and take proactive steps to identify, assess, and mitigate potential risks. This might involve diversifying suppliers, investing in technology to improve visibility in the supply chain, or developing contingency plans to ensure continuity in the face of disruptions.

In conclusion, while technology, processes, and systems are essential components of supply chain success, culture and leadership are equally important. A strong organizational culture that encourages collaboration, innovation, and accountability can significantly enhance the performance of the supply chain, making it more agile, efficient, and resilient. Similarly, effective leadership ensures that the supply chain strategy is aligned with the company's broader business goals and that teams are empowered to make decisions and take ownership of supply chain performance. In today's complex and competitive global market, companies that invest in building the right culture and leadership will be better positioned to achieve long-term success in their supply chain operations.

CHAPTER FOURTEEN
Measuring Supply Chain Performance and Continuous Improvement

Measuring supply chain performance is crucial to understanding the efficiency and effectiveness of operations, identifying areas of improvement, and making data-driven decisions that lead to competitive advantage. A well-functioning supply chain should not only meet the company's strategic objectives but also evolve continuously to adapt to market shifts, customer demands, and technological advancements. To achieve this, businesses must implement a structured approach to performance measurement, aligned with continuous improvement practices, ensuring that their supply chains remain agile, cost-efficient, and customer focused.

Supply chains are inherently complex, involving multiple stakeholders, processes, and external factors such as market volatility, regulatory requirements, and customer expectations. In this environment, it becomes essential to track performance at every level whether it's related to cost control, operational efficiency, supplier reliability, or customer satisfaction. However, many businesses still face challenges in determining which metrics to prioritize and how to use this data to drive actionable improvements. Measuring performance effectively involves more than just tracking numbers; it's about making the right measurements that align with strategic goals and ensuring that these insights lead to continuous improvement.

For companies to achieve sustained success, their supply chain measurement systems must be built around key performance indicators (KPIs) that reflect the company's unique objectives. While cost and service levels are common priorities, each company must tailor its performance metrics to specific business needs. For instance, a company focused on reducing lead times will prioritize speed and responsiveness, while another seeking to reduce environmental impact might focus on sustainability metrics. By tracking the right metrics, businesses can ensure that their supply chain activities are aligned with their broader goals, from enhancing customer experience to optimizing operational costs.

One of the primary metrics that businesses measure is cost. Supply chain costs have a direct impact on the bottom line, and understanding where expenses are occurring allows companies to find opportunities for cost reduction without compromising quality or service. Monitoring total supply chain costs, transportation and warehousing expenses, as well as procurement and manufacturing costs, helps companies gain visibility into their cost structure. This enables them to identify inefficiencies, such as high transportation costs due to suboptimal routing or excessive warehousing costs stemming from overstocking.

While controlling costs is important, businesses also need to measure service levels, which are critical to customer satisfaction. Delivering the right product to the customer on time and with high accuracy is essential to maintaining trust and building long-term relationships. Metrics such as on-time delivery rates, order accuracy, and order filling rates provide insight into how well a company meets customer expectations. If a business consistently fails to deliver on time or ships incorrect orders, it risks damaging its reputation, losing customers, and ultimately falling behind its competitors.

In addition to cost and service level metrics, inventory management is a critical component of supply chain performance. Inventory metrics help businesses strike the right balance between having enough stock to meet demand without tying up capital in excess inventory. Businesses that can manage their inventory efficiently reduce the risk of stockouts, which can lead to lost sales, and avoid overstocking, which increases holding costs. Inventory turnover, days of inventory on hand, and stockout rates are important metrics that provide visibility into inventory efficiency and help businesses ensure that their stock levels are aligned with customer demand.

Operational efficiency is another key area where performance measurement is essential. Supply chains that operate efficiently can reduce waste, improve production throughput, and enhance the speed and reliability of deliveries. Metrics such as cycle time, production efficiency, and capacity utilization allow businesses to monitor how well their operations are performing. Reducing cycle times, for example, enables companies to produce goods more quickly, improving time to market and increasing responsiveness to customer demand. Likewise, optimizing capacity utilization ensures that resources such as labor, machinery, and storage space are being used effectively.

Supplier performance is a critical factor in the overall success of the supply chain. Suppliers provide the raw materials and components necessary for production, and any disruption in their performance can have a ripple effect throughout the entire supply chain. To mitigate risks and ensure that suppliers meet expectations, businesses must track metrics such as lead times, quality defect rates, and supplier on-time performance. When suppliers consistently deliver high-quality goods on time, businesses can operate smoothly, avoiding delays and ensuring that customers receive their orders as expected. Conversely, poor supplier performance can lead to production delays, increased costs, and dissatisfied customers.

In recent years, sustainability has become a key focus area for many companies, driven by growing consumer awareness, regulatory requirements, and a commitment to corporate social responsibility. Measuring sustainability performance within the supply chain involves tracking metrics such as energy consumption, carbon emissions, and waste generation. Companies that monitor and actively work to reduce their environmental footprint not only meet the expectations of eco-conscious customers but also often uncover cost savings through energy efficiency and waste reduction initiatives. For instance, by optimizing transportation routes or investing in more energy-efficient machinery, businesses can reduce both their carbon footprint and fuel costs.

Once a company has established the relevant KPIs for its supply chain, the next step is ensuring that these metrics are reviewed regularly and acted upon. Supply chain performance should not be static; instead, it should be subject to continuous monitoring and refinement. This is where the concept of continuous improvement comes into play. Continuous improvement is an ongoing effort to enhance processes, systems, and outcomes. In the context of supply chain management, it involves regularly evaluating performance data, identifying areas where improvements can be made, implementing changes, and then reassessing performance to ensure that those changes had the desired effect.

To embed continuous improvement into supply chain management, businesses need to foster a culture that encourages proactive problem-solving and innovation. Employees at all levels of the organization should be empowered to contribute ideas for improving processes, whether it's reducing lead times, streamlining inventory management, or optimizing transportation. Leaders play a crucial role in promoting this culture by providing the tools, resources, and support necessary for employees to take ownership of supply chain performance. When employees feel engaged and empowered, they are more likely to look for ways to enhance efficiency, improve customer satisfaction, and reduce costs.

In addition to fostering a culture of improvement, businesses must use data analytics to support continuous improvement initiatives. Modern supply chains generate vast amounts of data, and by leveraging data analytics tools, businesses can gain deeper insights into the performance of their supply chain. Predictive analytics, for example, can help businesses forecast demand more accurately, reduce stockouts, and optimize inventory levels. Advanced analytics can also uncover inefficiencies in logistics and transportation, allowing companies to adjust routes, consolidate shipments, or negotiate better rates with carriers. By making data-driven decisions, businesses can implement changes with greater confidence and measure their impact more effectively.

Collaboration is another critical factor in achieving continuous improvement in the supply chain. Supply chains are highly interconnected, with multiple stakeholders, including suppliers, manufacturers, logistics providers, and customers. To achieve lasting improvements, businesses must work closely with these partners, sharing data, aligning objectives, and co-developing solutions. When businesses and suppliers collaborate, for instance, they can jointly identify ways to improve product quality, reduce lead times, or innovate more sustainable production methods. Such collaboration leads to more integrated and efficient supply chains, where all parties benefit from shared improvements.

One of the challenges of continuous improvement in supply chain management is managing change. Change, even when intended to improve performance, can be disruptive, especially in complex, global supply chains. It's important for businesses to implement change management strategies that ensure a smooth transition whenever new processes, technologies, or performance goals are introduced. Change management involves clear communication, training, and support to ensure that all stakeholders understand the rationale behind the changes, how the changes will be implemented, and what role they will play in achieving success.

In conclusion, measuring supply chain performance is a fundamental component of effective supply chain management. By tracking relevant KPIs related to cost, service levels, inventory management, operational efficiency, supplier performance, and sustainability, businesses can gain the visibility they need to optimize their supply chains. However, measurement alone is not enough. To remain competitive, companies must adopt a continuous improvement mindset, using performance data to drive ongoing enhancements, foster innovation, and collaborate with partners. With the right metrics, a commitment to improvement, and a focus on collaboration, businesses can build agile, efficient, and resilient supply chains that are well-positioned for long-term success.

CHAPTER FIFTEEN
Future Trends in Global Supply Chain Management

The future of global supply chain management is being shaped by a convergence of technological advancements, shifting consumer expectations, environmental imperatives, and evolving geopolitical dynamics. As businesses navigate an increasingly complex and interconnected world, supply chains must adapt to remain competitive. The companies that thrive in this changing landscape will be those that embrace innovation, harness emerging technologies, and build resilient, agile supply chains capable of responding to both challenges and opportunities.

One of the most significant trends shaping the future of supply chain management is the continued rise of digitalization. The integration of digital technologies, such as artificial intelligence (AI), machine learning, blockchain, and the Internet of Things (IoT), is transforming how supply chains operate. These technologies provide real-time visibility, enhance decision-making, and automate processes, making supply chains more efficient and responsive.

AI and machine learning, for example, are being used to predict demand patterns with greater accuracy, enabling businesses to optimize their inventory levels and reduce waste. Machine learning algorithms can analyze historical sales data, external market factors, and even social media trends to forecast demand and adjust supply chain operations accordingly. This helps companies avoid overproduction, reduce holding costs, and ensure that the right products are available when and where customers need them.

Blockchain technology is also playing a transformative role in supply chain management by improving transparency and security. Blockchain allows businesses to create a decentralized, tamper-proof record of transactions, ensuring that all stakeholders have access to a single source of truth. This is particularly valuable in industries such as food, pharmaceuticals, and luxury goods, where traceability and authenticity are critical. With blockchain, companies can verify the origin of raw materials, track the movement of goods through the supply chain, and ensure that products meet regulatory and ethical standards.

The IoT is another game-changing technology that is reshaping supply chains. IoT devices, such as sensors and RFID tags, enable businesses to track the location, condition, and status of goods in real time. This level of visibility allows companies to monitor inventory levels, prevent stockouts, and ensure that products are stored and transported under optimal conditions. For example, sensors can monitor the temperature and humidity of perishable goods during transportation, ensuring that they remain within acceptable parameters. If any deviations occur, the system can automatically trigger alerts, allowing businesses to take corrective action before the product is damaged.

Sustainability is another critical trend that will continue to shape the future of supply chain management. Consumers, regulators, and investors are placing increasing pressure on businesses to reduce their environmental impact and adopt more sustainable practices. Supply chains are a significant source of carbon emissions, waste, and resource consumption, making sustainability a top priority for companies looking to enhance their environmental credentials and meet regulatory requirements.

To build more sustainable supply chains, businesses are investing in green technologies, such as electric vehicles for transportation, renewable energy sources, and more sustainable packaging materials. Companies are also working with suppliers to reduce waste, minimize resource use, and improve the sustainability of their supply chains. In addition, many businesses are exploring circular supply chain models, where products and materials are reused, refurbished, or recycled rather than being discarded. By adopting circular supply chain practices, companies can reduce waste, lower costs, and create new revenue streams through the resale or repurposing of products.

Geopolitical and economic shifts are another major force shaping the future of global supply chains. Trade wars, tariffs, regulatory changes, and political instability can disrupt supply chains and increase costs. As a result, businesses are rethinking their supply chain strategies to reduce their exposure to geopolitical risks. This may involve diversifying their supplier base, reshoring production, or establishing regional supply chains that are less dependent on global trade routes. The COVID-19 pandemic has also underscored the importance of supply chain resilience, prompting many companies to build greater flexibility and redundancy into their supply chains to better withstand future disruptions.

Automation is another key trend that is transforming global supply chains. Advances in robotics, autonomous vehicles, and warehouse automation are enabling businesses to streamline their operations, reduce labor costs, and improve efficiency. For example, automated warehouses equipped with robots can pick, pack, and ship orders much faster and more accurately than human workers. Autonomous vehicles, such as self-driving trucks and drones, are also being used to improve transportation efficiency and reduce delivery times, particularly in last-mile delivery.

The future of supply chain management will also be shaped by the increasing importance of data. As supply chains generate more data than ever before, businesses must find ways to harness this data to make smarter decisions and drive continuous improvement. Advanced analytics, predictive modeling, and real-time monitoring tools will be essential for gaining actionable insights from the vast amounts of data generated by supply chain activities. Companies that can leverage data effectively will be better positioned to optimize their operations, improve customer satisfaction, and stay ahead of the competition.

In conclusion, the future of global supply chain management is being shaped by a combination of technological advancements, sustainability imperatives, geopolitical dynamics, and the increasing importance of data. To remain competitive, businesses must embrace these trends and invest in building supply chains that are agile, resilient, and responsive to changing market conditions. By leveraging emerging technologies, adopting sustainable practices, and building greater flexibility into their operations, companies can create supply chains that are not only efficient and cost-effective but also future-ready. In an increasingly complex and interconnected world, the ability to adapt and innovate will be the key to supply chain success in the years to come.

Soviet and Post-Soviet Politics and Society (SPPS)   Vol. 149
ISSN 1614-3515

General Editor: Andreas Umland,
Institute for Euro-Atlantic Cooperation, Kyiv, umland@stanfordalumni.org

Commissioning Editor: Max Jakob Horstmann,
London, mjh@ibidem.eu

EDITORIAL COMMITTEE*

DOMESTIC & COMPARATIVE POLITICS
Prof. **Ellen Bos**, *Andrássy University of Budapest*
Dr. **Ingmar Bredies**, *FH Bund, Brühl*
Dr. **Andrey Kazantsev**, *MGIMO (U) MID RF, Moscow*
Prof. **Heiko Pleines**, *University of Bremen*
Prof. **Richard Sakwa**, *University of Kent at Canterbury*
Dr. **Sarah Whitmore**, *Oxford Brookes University*
Dr. **Harald Wydra**, *University of Cambridge*

SOCIETY, CLASS & ETHNICITY
Col. **David Glantz**, *"Journal of Slavic Military Studies"*
Dr. **Marlène Laruelle**, *George Washington University*
Dr. **Stephen Shulman**, *Southern Illinois University*
Prof. **Stefan Troebst**, *University of Leipzig*

POLITICAL ECONOMY & PUBLIC POLICY
Prof. em. **Marshall Goldman**, *Wellesley College, Mass.*
Dr. **Andreas Goldthau**, *Central European University*
Dr. **Robert Kravchuk**, *University of North Carolina*
Dr. **David Lane**, *University of Cambridge*
Dr. **Carol Leonard**, *Higher School of Economics, Moscow*
Dr. **Maria Popova**, *McGill University, Montreal*

FOREIGN POLICY & INTERNATIONAL AFFAIRS
Dr. **Peter Duncan**, *University College London*
Prof. **Andreas Heinemann-Grüder**, *University of Bonn*
Dr. **Taras Kuzio**, *Johns Hopkins University*
Prof. **Gerhard Mangott**, *University of Innsbruck*
Dr. **Diana Schmidt-Pfister**, *University of Konstanz*
Dr. **Lisbeth Tarlow**, *Harvard University, Cambridge*
Dr. **Christian Wipperfürth**, *N-Ost Network, Berlin*
Dr. **William Zimmerman**, *University of Michigan*

HISTORY, CULTURE & THOUGHT
Dr. **Catherine Andreyev**, *University of Oxford*
Prof. **Mark Bassin**, *Södertörn University*
Prof. **Karsten Brüggemann**, *Tallinn University*
Dr. **Alexander Etkind**, *University of Cambridge*
Dr. **Gasan Gusejnov**, *Moscow State University*
Prof. em. **Walter Laqueur**, *Georgetown University*
Prof. **Leonid Luks**, *Catholic University of Eichstaett*
Dr. **Olga Malinova**, *Russian Academy of Sciences*
Prof. **Andrei Rogatchevski**, *University of Tromsø*
Dr. **Mark Tauger**, *West Virginia University*

ADVISORY BOARD*

Prof. **Dominique Arel**, *University of Ottawa*
Prof. **Jörg Baberowski**, *Humboldt University of Berlin*
Prof. **Margarita Balmaceda**, *Seton Hall University*
Dr. **John Barber**, *University of Cambridge*
Prof. **Timm Beichelt**, *European University Viadrina*
Dr. **Katrin Boeckh**, *University of Munich*
Prof. em. **Archie Brown**, *University of Oxford*
Dr. **Vyacheslav Bryukhovetsky**, *Kyiv-Mohyla Academy*
Prof. **Timothy Colton**, *Harvard University, Cambridge*
Prof. **Paul D'Anieri**, *University of Florida*
Dr. **Heike Dörrenbächer**, *Friedrich Naumann Foundation*
Dr. **John Dunlop**, *Hoover Institution, Stanford, California*
Dr. **Sabine Fischer**, *SWP, Berlin*
Dr. **Geir Flikke**, *NUPI, Oslo*
Prof. **David Galbreath**, *University of Aberdeen*
Prof. **Alexander Galkin**, *Russian Academy of Sciences*
Prof. **Frank Golczewski**, *University of Hamburg*
Dr. **Nikolas Gvosdev**, *Naval War College, Newport, RI*
Prof. **Mark von Hagen**, *Arizona State University*
Dr. **Guido Hausmann**, *University of Munich*
Prof. **Dale Herspring**, *Kansas State University*
Dr. **Stefani Hoffman**, *Hebrew University of Jerusalem*
Prof. **Mikhail Ilyin**, *MGIMO (U) MID RF, Moscow*
Prof. **Vladimir Kantor**, *Higher School of Economics*
Dr. **Ivan Katchanovski**, *University of Ottawa*
Prof. em. **Andrzej Korbonski**, *University of California*
Dr. **Iris Kempe**, *"Caucasus Analytical Digest"*
Prof. **Herbert Küpper**, *Institut für Ostrecht Regensburg*
Dr. **Rainer Lindner**, *CEEER, Berlin*
Dr. **Vladimir Malakhov**, *Russian Academy of Sciences*

Dr. **Luke March**, *University of Edinburgh*
Prof. **Michael McFaul**, *Stanford University, Palo Alto*
Prof. **Birgit Menzel**, *University of Mainz-Germersheim*
Prof. **Valery Mikhailenko**, *The Urals State University*
Prof. **Emil Pain**, *Higher School of Economics, Moscow*
Dr. **Oleg Podvintsev**, *Russian Academy of Sciences*
Prof. **Olga Popova**, *St. Petersburg State University*
Dr. **Alex Pravda**, *University of Oxford*
Dr. **Erik van Ree**, *University of Amsterdam*
Dr. **Joachim Rogall**, *Robert Bosch Foundation Stuttgart*
Prof. **Peter Rutland**, *Wesleyan University, Middletown*
Prof. **Marat Salikov**, *The Urals State Law Academy*
Dr. **Gwendolyn Sasse**, *University of Oxford*
Prof. **Jutta Scherrer**, *EHESS, Paris*
Prof. **Robert Service**, *University of Oxford*
Mr. **James Sherr**, *RIIA Chatham House London*
Dr. **Oxana Shevel**, *Tufts University, Medford*
Prof. **Eberhard Schneider**, *University of Siegen*
Prof. **Olexander Shnyrkov**, *Shevchenko University, Kyiv*
Prof. **Hans-Henning Schröder**, *SWP, Berlin*
Prof. **Yuri Shapoval**, *Ukrainian Academy of Sciences*
Prof. **Viktor Shnirelman**, *Russian Academy of Sciences*
Dr. **Lisa Sundstrom**, *University of British Columbia*
Dr. **Philip Walters**, *"Religion, State and Society", Oxford*
Prof. **Zenon Wasyliw**, *Ithaca College, New York State*
Dr. **Lucan Way**, *University of Toronto*
Dr. **Markus Wehner**, *"Frankfurter Allgemeine Zeitung"*
Dr. **Andrew Wilson**, *University College London*
Prof. **Jan Zielonka**, *University of Oxford*
Prof. **Andrei Zorin**, *University of Oxford*

* While the Editorial Committee and Advisory Board support the General Editor in the choice and improvement of manuscripts for publication, responsibility for remaining errors and misinterpretations in the series' volumes lies with the books' authors.

Soviet and Post-Soviet Politics and Society (SPPS)
ISSN 1614-3515

Founded in 2004 and refereed since 2007, SPPS makes available affordable English-, German-, and Russian-language studies on the history of the countries of the former Soviet bloc from the late Tsarist period to today. It publishes between 5 and 20 volumes per year and focuses on issues in transitions to and from democracy such as economic crisis, identity formation, civil society development, and constitutional reform in CEE and the NIS. SPPS also aims to highlight so far understudied themes in East European studies such as right-wing radicalism, religious life, higher education, or human rights protection. The authors and titles of all previously published volumes are listed at the end of this book. For a full description of the series and reviews of its books, see www.ibidem-verlag.de/red/spps.

Editorial correspondence & manuscripts should be sent to: Dr. Andreas Umland, c/o DAAD, German Embassy, vul. Bohdana Khmelnitskoho 25, UA-01901 Kyiv, Ukraine. e-mail: umland@stanfordalumni.org

Business correspondence & review copy requests should be sent to: *ibidem* Press, Leuschnerstr. 40, 30457 Hannover, Germany; tel.: +49 511 2622200; fax: +49 511 2622201; spps@ibidem.eu.

Authors, reviewers, referees, and editors for (as well as all other persons sympathetic to) SPPS are invited to join its networks at www.facebook.com/group.php?gid=52638198614
www.linkedin.com/groups?about=&gid=103012
www.xing.com/net/spps-ibidem-verlag/

Recent Volumes

143   Инна Чувычкина (ред.)
Экспортные нефте- и газопроводы на постсоветском пространстве
Анализ трубопроводной политики в свете теории международных отношений
ISBN 978-3-8382-0822-0

144   Johann Zajaczkowski
Russland – eine pragmatische Großmacht?
Eine rollentheoretische Untersuchung russischer Außenpolitik am Beispiel der Zusammenarbeit mit den USA nach 9/11 und des Georgienkrieges von 2008
Mit einem Vorwort von Siegfried Schieder
ISBN 978-3-8382-0837-4

145   Boris Popivanov
Changing Images of the Left in Bulgaria
The Challenge of Post-Communism in the Early 21st Century
ISBN 978-3-8382-0667-7

146   Lenka Krátká
A History of the Czechoslovak Ocean Shipping Company 1948-1989
How a Small, Landlocked Country Ran Maritime Business During the Cold War
ISBN 978-3-8382-0666-0

147   Alexander Sergunin
Explaining Russian Foreign Policy Behavior
Theory and Practice
ISBN 978-3-8382-0752-0

148   Darya Malyutina
Migrant Friendships in a Super-Diverse City
Russian-Speakers and their Social Relationships in London in the 21st Century
With a foreword by Claire Dwyer
ISBN 978-3-8382-0652-3

149   Alexander Sergunin, Valery Konyshev
Russia in the Arctic
Hard or Soft Power?
ISBN 978-3-8382-0753-7

150   John J. Maresca
Helsinki Revisited
A Key U.S. Negotiator's Memoirs on the Development of the CSCE into the OSCE
With a foreword by Hafiz Pashayev
ISBN 978-3-8382-0852-7